Cuneiform

Cover A tablet of the Jemdet Nasr period. BM 116730. (See also p. 53.)

1 Neo-Babylonian stone monument commemorating Adad-eṭir and his son
Marduk-balassu-iqbi. BM 90834.

Cuneiform

C. B. F. Walker

University of California Press/British Museum

University of California Press
Berkeley and Los Angeles California

© 1987 The Trustees of the British Museum

Designed by Arthur Lockwood
Front cover design by Grahame Dudley

Printed in Great Britain

Volume 3 in the *Reading The past* series

Library of Congress Cataloguing-in-Publication Data
Walker, C. B. F.
  Cuneiform.

  (Reading the past)
  Bibliography: p.
  Includes index.
  1. Cuneiform writing. I. Title. II. Series.
PJ3193.W35 1988   417′.7   87-5879
ISBN 0-520-06115-2 (pbk.)

Preface

Cuneiform writing was for 2,500 years one of the two principal media of literate civilisation, together with Egyptian hieroglyphs. If one adds the 500 years of its slow decline then it matches the length of time for which our own alphabet has been in common use. It is beyond the scope of this book to give even a brief sketch of the history of the different peoples and kingdoms involved. The maps and chronological table, however, are designed to give a basic outline. In any case, our knowledge of the details of chronology often remains inadequate, so many events or changes can only be dated generally to centuries or millennia.

Archaeologists and historians alike have tended to be quite inconsistent in their use of place names, ancient or modern. So, to avoid confusion, I have kept to the ancient names where known, giving the modern names in brackets where common usage has made them well known. Since much of the subject matter is common to the civilisations of Sumer, Babylon and Assyria I frequently use the term Mesopotamia to cover all three.

Assyrian and Babylonian are both dialects of the Akkadian language, and I use all three terms. Transliterations of Akkadian are printed in italic script, while Sumerian is printed in Roman upper or lower case, and translations are printed in quotes.

C. B. F. Walker

1
Origin and Development

Pictographs

Writing was invented in order to record business activities in the early Near East. With the growth of centralised economies the officials of palaces and temples needed to be able to keep track of the amounts of grain and numbers of sheep and cattle which were entering or leaving their stores and farms. It was impossible to rely on a man's memory for every detail, and a new method was needed to keep reliable records.

When man first began to write he wrote not with pen and ink on paper but by scratching signs on to damp clay with a pointed stick or reed. The raw materials were readily available in the river valleys of the Near East and cost little effort to prepare. Clay can be easily worked into a suitably flat shape for writing on while moist, and if left to dry in the sun after being inscribed will soon be hard enough to stand up to considerable wear and tear.

On the very earliest texts pictures (sometimes called pictographs) were drawn on damp clay using a pointed tool. But quite soon the scribes found it was quicker to produce a stylised representation of an object by making a few marks in the clay rather than attempt an artistic impression by naturalistic drawing in straight or curving lines. These stylised representations then had to be standardised so that everyone could recognise them. Since the scribes were no longer trying to be great artists the drawing instrument did not have to be finely pointed but could be blunt or flat. The end of the wooden or reed stylus, which struck the clay first, made a wider mark than the shaft, and so came into being the typical wedge-shaped impression after which this writing system became known – cuneiform (from the Latin word *cuneus* meaning wedge). Many early tablets show a mixture of signs drawn and written in cuneiform.

Until quite recently the theory presented in most books on Mesopotamian archaeology was that writing was invented in southern Iraq *c*. 3000 BC, or slightly earlier, perhaps by a Sumerian living in Uruk. Whether or not he was Sumerian is uncertain since the very earliest texts of all are purely pictographic (picture writing) and without phonetic indications to show which language is being written. The suggestion that he lived in Uruk was based on the facts that the earliest evidence for writing was found there and that by 3000 BC the city had already enjoyed a long history.

Today the picture looks rather different. Evidence for early stages of writing in the form of tablets inscribed with numbers only, sometimes also bearing seal impressions, has been found not only at Uruk but also at Nineveh in Iraq, at Susa, Choga Mish and Godin Tepe in western Iran, and at Tell Brak and Habuba Kabira in north Syria; most of these can be dated to the later fourth millennium BC. Next, two tablets from Tell Brak, found in 1984, depict a goat and a sheep, each accompanied by the number 10. They are quite as primitive as anything from Uruk; if anything they may even be earlier, since they show the whole of the animals, whereas pictures on the earliest tablets from Uruk show only the heads of animals. In the east the pictographic texts found at Susa, known as

8

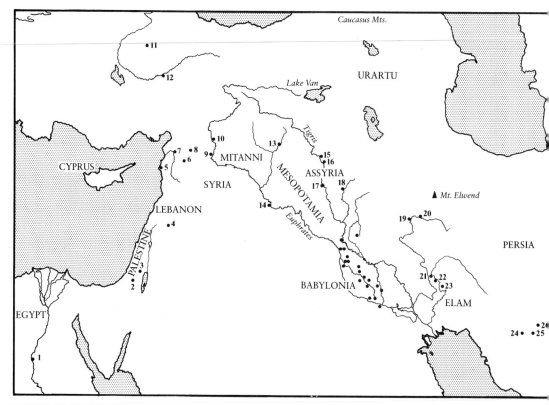

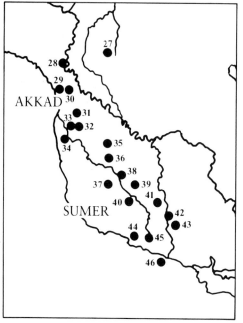

Above The Middle East.
Left Babylonia.

1 El-Amarna	24 Tall-i-Malyan
2 Lachish	25 Persepolis
3 Jerusalem	26 Pasargadae
4 Damascus	27 Eshnunna
5 Ugarit	28 Baghdad
6 Ebla	29 Sippar
7 Alalakh	30 Tell ed-Der
8 Aleppo	31 Jemdet Nasr
9 Habuba Kabira	32 Kish
10 Til Barsip	33 Babylon
11 Hattusas	34 Borsippa
12 Kanesh	35 Abu Salabikh
13 Brak	36 Nippur
14 Mari	37 Isin
15 Nineveh	38 Puzrish-Dagan
16 Kalhu	39 Adab
17 Ashur	40 Shuruppak
18 Nuzi	41 Umma
19 Behistun	42 Girsu
20 Godin Tepe	43 Lagash
21 Susa	44 Uruk
22 Dur-Untash	45 Larsa
23 Choga Mish	46 Ur

2 Pictographic tablets from Tell Brak.

proto-Elamite, appear in an archaeological level which shows marked differences from the previous level, suggesting the arrival of a new cultural group, and since these proto-Elamite texts have now been found as far east as Seistan on the border of Afghanistan, it may be that the script was invented on the Iranian plateau. Study of the early Uruk texts themselves has also suggested that they are dependent on an earlier tradition of pictography which has not yet been found or identified. Thus it is beginning to look as if we should think in terms of the invention of writing as being a gradual process, accomplished over a wide area, rather than the product of a single Sumerian genius.

In practice any meaningful discussion has to start with the tablets found at Uruk in the early archaeological level known as Uruk IV and a slightly later group found in Uruk III. Contemporary with the Uruk III tablets are tablets from Jemdet Nasr to the north and the proto-Elamite tablets from Susa. Historically the Uruk IV–III levels date to *c.* 3300 – 2900 BC. There are both similarities and differences between the tablets from Uruk and Jemdet Nasr and those from Susa, but while the Uruk and Jemdet Nasr tablets are regarded as the beginning of writing in Sumerian, the Susa tablets are seen as the first examples of the still little-understood Elamite language.

3 A proto-Elamite tablet.
Musée du Louvre, Paris.

10

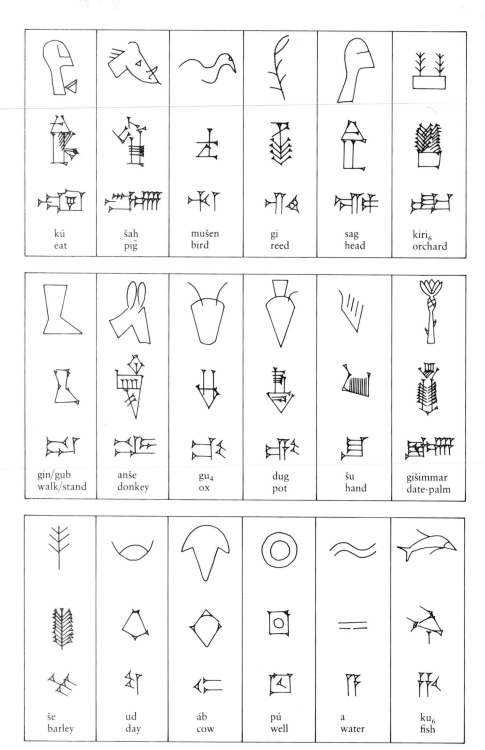

4 Table of cuneiform signs showing for each sign the pictographic form (*c.* 3000 BC), an early cuneiform representation (*c.* 2400 BC), and the Late Assyrian form (*c.* 650 BC), now turned through 90 degrees, with the Sumerian phonetic equivalent and meaning.

The inscriptions on these early tablets consist of brief economic records or lists of signs for the instruction of trainee scribes. The signs are mostly pictographic: that is to say the sign for an ox looks like an ox's head, the sign for barley looks like an ear of barley, and the sign for a day is a picture of the sun coming up over the horizon. The pictures quickly take on a cuneiform appearance and are regularly accompanied by numbers, which is enough to suggest that the texts were economic (receipts, delivery notes or inventories). An intensive study of all these early texts by a team from the University of Berlin from a mathematical point of view is slowly producing a better understanding of the meaning of the texts and the nature of the underlying economic system, although we are still a long way from being able to read the texts rather than interpret them.

Eighty-five per cent of the tablets from the early levels at Uruk are economic and are concerned with the income and outgoings of the city's temples in terms of food, live-stock and textiles. Remarkably, it has been possible to identify a large number of place names known from the later history of Sumer, mostly within the vicinity of Uruk, but including Kish and Eshnunna to the north, Aratta (somewhere in the mountains of Iran), and Dilmun (modern Bahrein). Fifteen per cent of the texts are lexical lists, including the names of various commodities, animals and officials. These lists were presumably compiled to establish and teach a definitive system of writing recognisable to every scribe. Significantly, exactly the same lists can be found from six hundred years later, showing the strength of the tradition. This continuity has been a great help in identi-fying many of the early signs which would otherwise have been quite unintelligible. Popular books on cuneiform have tended to give the impression that identifying the early signs is easy; in fact things are not so simple. Pictures of an ox or an ear of barley are identifiable, but there are many signs which we cannot yet explain as pictures even when by working back from the later lexical lists we are able to establish their meaning.

As soon as we are able to read the texts intelligibly, we are confronted by another difficulty. The early texts are not written in neat lines with every sign in the appropriate order – that came later – but with all the signs for each sense unit (or sentence) grouped together in a box (see front cover). The correct order in which to read the signs is thus a matter of interpretation.

Syllabic writing

The texts from Uruk and Jemdet Nasr, although slowly changing from a pictorial to a more linear or cuneiform script, are still largely logographic, that is to say that they use one sign or sign-group for each term or concept without adding grammatical elements. Even the nature of a transaction is not always clear; are the sheep being brought into or out of the temple? We do not know. In any case how could they tell us? Drawing an ox's head to represent an ox is straightforward. But how do you say that the ox is live or dead? How do you record that it has come or gone? And how do you record the name of the person who brought or took it? To communicate these things effectively you need to do more than draw pictures. You have to be able to express ideas. You have to be able to record a spoken language. The alphabet was not invented until 1,500 years later, so the first scribes used syllables instead.

This syllabic stage of the script's development is known from a group of texts from Ur corresponding to the archaeological levels Early Dynastic I–II (c. 2800 BC). In these

5 An archaic tablet from Ur,
c. 2900–2600 BC;
deliveries of barley and
meal to a temple.
BM 128897.

6 (*Opposite*) A tablet of the Fara
type (*c.* 2600 BC); a record of
numbers of workmen.
BM 21014.

texts we find the first identifiable use of purely phonetic elements and grammar, and as soon as we are able to identify the use of syllables in the cuneiform script we encounter the Sumerian language. The Sumerians may have been responsible for introducing writing at Uruk, but it cannot be proved. Because the script does not perfectly suit all the sounds which linguistic experts find in Sumerian, it has been suggested that the cuneiform script was devised by another people. In any case their origins are uncertain, and they have in the past been thought of as invaders from the eastern mountains. On the other hand the relative cultural continuity in the late Uruk period has suggested to others that the Sumerians were there all along.

| še | gu | gú/gu₂ | gù/gu₃ | gu₄ | ti | ud |

In Sumerian the word for barley is še (pronounced 'she' as in shepherd), so the sign for barley also became the sign for the syllable še. The Sumerian for ox is gu; but the word for thread is also gu, so already you have two possible ways of writing the sound gu. There are, in fact, some fourteen ways of writing gu, so for convenience we (but not the ancient Sumerians) mark thread as gu and ox as gu₄. The word for arrow is ti, but so is the word for life, so to write 'life' you need only write the sign for arrow. The word for mouth is ka (represented as a head with the teeth clearly marked), but the sign ka is also used for the idea of shouting, which is again gu (gu₃ or gù); so the sign KA already has two values, ka and gu₃ (and in fact it can also be used for zú 'tooth', du₁₁ 'speak', and inim 'word'). Combining a syllable formed of consonant + vowel (like gu) with one formed from vowel + consonant (like ud 'day') allows you to make a closed syllable, gu-ud. In this way you can make up any combination of vowels and consonants, so long as you do not want to put more than two consonants together (no Sumerian cartoonist could write 'Psst!'). The principle of using several signs to represent the same sound (gu) is called homophony, and giving one sign several values (like KA) is called polyphony. Both principles are fundamental features of cuneiform writing throughout its 3,000 year history.

The early stages of Sumerian writing represented by tablets from Uruk, Jemdet Nasr

and Ur contain no historical material and generally fall outside the scope of historical discussion, being dated solely by archaeological considerations. The only history available for this period is in the form of a later tradition listing kings who lived before the Flood. With the next group of material we enter recorded history in what is known as the Early Dynastic period (II – III). Enmebaragesi, king of Kish (c. 2600 BC), is the first man known to be commemorated by his own inscription (to be seen in the Iraq Museum, Baghdad). Roughly contemporary with him are the tablets from Shuruppak (Fara), known in Sumerian literature as the home of the Sumerian Flood-hero Ziusudra. The tablets from Fara and the slightly later archives from Abu Salabikh and Ebla (in Syria) show the gradual development of the Sumerian script both in the form of the signs and in the flexibility of its use.

From these three cities come the first major groups of literary texts, including what one might call the first autographs in history, tablets on which the scribes have recorded their own names. The tablets from Abu Salabikh and Ebla show that literature and the study of cuneiform vocabulary were already highly developed. Slightly later again come the administrative archives from Girsu (Tello) and with these we also have a wealth of historical inscriptions to complete the setting. The Early Dynastic III period ends with the accession of Sargon of Akkad (2334–2279 BC), and the beginning of a strong Akkadian influence in politics and language. The Akkadian language is discussed below, but we should consider now one fundamental change in the writing system which seems to have taken place late in the Early Dynastic period – the change in the direction of writing.

The direction of the script

The pictographs on the earliest tablets are clearly meant to be read as naturalistic pictures. But when one traces their development through time it becomes apparent that at some point they have been turned through ninety degrees so that they are lying on their backs. The same applies to the overall direction of the script. The Uruk and Jemdet Nasr texts are mostly written on slightly elongated tablets, wider than they are high. The signs are disposed randomly within squares or rectangles. The rectangles are arranged in rows to be read from right to left, and when one row is filled a new row is started beneath it. When the front of the tablet is full up, the tablet is turned left to right and the back of the tablet is inscribed in the same manner but starting from the bottom up. In contrast by 2000 BC tablets are mostly higher than they are wide, and are inscribed with the signs written in order from left to right in long lines. In many cases there is only a single column of script on each face of the tablet, although on some Sumerian texts of the Ur III period (2112–2004 BC) there can be up to eleven columns on each side.

It had been thought that the change in direction of the script took place as early as the Jemdet Nasr period. It was also suggested that the change arose because scribes writing from right to left found they were smudging their handiwork; practical experience in writing cuneiform on clay shows, however, that with good quality clay very little smudging takes place and a conscious effort is needed to erase signs. More importantly, there are historical arguments against an early change in the direction of writing. Until the middle of the second millennium most stone monuments and all inscribed cylinder seals preserve the archaic direction of script. So in reading the inscription on the great law code of Hammurapi one has to hold one's head down on the right shoulder. The direction of the script is obviously intended to preserve an ancient tradition, but it could hardly have become traditional if the direction of writing had changed already in the Jemdet Nasr period before any monumental inscriptions had been written.

The late Adam Falkenstein argued for a change at the end of the Early Dynastic period since some of the tablets from Girsu dated to that period have drawings of animals which can only be viewed the right way up if the script is read as in early times. This seems to be a forceful argument, although there is at least one stone monument from the late Early Dynastic (BM 117936 in the British Museum) which shows three standing figures and an inscription (still only partly legible) which must be read in the later direction (horizontally). There is another small point which seems to have been overlooked up to now. The earliest tablets inscribed in a single column date to the time of Lugalzagesi, king of Uruk, the contemporary and predecessor of Sargon. This too suggests that the change had taken place shortly before. What induced it and how it was imposed remain obscure. One consequence was a reduction in the variety of wedges used to form signs. When read from the direction later customary, many signs used on Early Dynastic tablets have wedges pointing vertically upwards. From Old Akkadian times on, these wedges are almost entirely eliminated, so that the heads of wedges appear only at the top or the left side of a sign.

šu   da   ru   níg

7 A tablet of the time of Lugalzagesi, king of Uruk (2340–2316 BC). BM 114362.

It may be that the change seemed less significant to the ancient scribes than it does to us. Writing on a small tablet with the tablet held in one hand and the stylus held in the other is a two-handed operation, turning the tablet to impress wedges in different directions. Thus the scribes would have become used to seeing their writing from more than one angle. At all events the scribes of the Ur III and Old Babylonian periods must have been well accustomed to reading public monuments inscribed in the older direction. Today scholars are so familiar with the later direction of the script that most early tablets are published and exhibited the wrong way round.

Sumerian and Akkadian

So far the cuneiform script has been discussed only with reference to Sumerian. From the mid-third millennium onwards it was also used to write the Akkadian language in southern Mesopotamia and the Eblaite language at Ebla in Syria (see Chapter 4). So it may be helpful at this point to make some brief remarks on the nature of the Sumerian and Akkadian languages and the way in which the cuneiform script was used to record them.

The Sumerian language first became known from bilingual texts written in Sumerian and Akkadian and found in the seventh-century BC royal libraries at Nineveh. For some time many scholars refused even to believe that it was a language at all and suggested that it was a scribal trick or a form of cryptography. The discovery of vast archives inscribed unilingually in Sumerian put paid to that idea. The early doubters may, however, be forgiven since Sumerian is quite unlike the well-known Indo-European and Semitic language groups.

Linguists describe the language as agglutinative; each fundamental idea, nominal or verbal, is expressed by a single unchanging syllable (or polysyllable) which may be modified by a series of prefixes or postfixes, somewhat as in modern Turkish. Thus 'son' is dumu, 'sons' dumu-meš, 'his sons' dumu-meš-a-ni, 'for his sons' dumu-meš-a-ni-ir (for explanation of š see p. 12). The verb 'build' is dù, 'he built' ì-dù or mu-dù, 'he did not build' nu-mu-dù. So 'For Ningirsu his god Gudea built his temple' is Ningirsu dingir-ra-ni-ir Gudea é-a-ni mu-dù. So far so good, but the scribes were hardly consistent in their implementation of the system. In fact in the early periods many of the verbal prefixes and postfixes were not written at all; the sign dù expressed the idea 'build' and the rest had to be supplied by the reader. In some respects the Sumerian script never quite escapes from the fact that it was originally designed for the purpose of practical book-keeping rather than to express abstract ideas. When we reach the Old Babylonian period (2004–1595 BC), the time when most of the available literary texts were copied, we find that many duplicates of these texts use different groups of prefixes or postfixes. That does not make it easy to write a grammar of Sumerian.

The Sumerian language uses only four vowels: a, e, i, u; two half vowels: w and y; and the following consonants: b, d, g, k, l, m, n, p, r, s, t, z, ḫ, g̃, š. The ḫ corresponds to a hard h, g̃ is a nasalised g, and š corresponds to English sh.

In addition to writing out a text phonetically the Sumerian scribes gave themselves extra clues for their own decipherment by adding certain specific signs to mark different categories of objects. So wooden objects might have the prefix giš, stone objects na$_4$, copper objects urudu, cities uru; birds have the postfix mušen, fish ku$_6$, cities ki (some cities are even uru-X-ki).

If all of this seems complicated, matters get worse when one tries to use the Sumerian system for the Akkadian language, for which it was not designed and to which it is not well suited.

Akkadian is one of the Semitic languages, together with Arabic, Hebrew, Aramaic, etc. It has three dialects: Old Akkadian, Babylonian and Assyrian; so by definition anything written in Babylonian or Assyrian can equally be said to be written in Akkadian. Each of these dialects tends to use a slightly variant form of the cuneiform script, although all handbooks to cuneiform take them as one. As in the other Semitic languages, Akkadian words basically have a root of three consonants, e.g. *prs*, which is then modified internally by the doubling of consonants or insertion of vowels, and externally by the addition of prefixes or postfixes, e.g. *iprus*, *purus*, *iparrasūni*. Thus in principle no single cuneiform sign could carry the meaning of an Akkadian word, and the practical solution was to write words out phonetically. To a large extent this happened, but additionally Akkadian-speaking scribes used Sumerian signs to express Akkadian terms, e.g. Sumerian udu-meš for Akkadian *immerū*, 'sheep', or mixed the two, e.g. Sumerian gal = 'great', but gal-*u* = Akkadian *rabû*, 'great'. (For clarity Assyriologists write Sumerian in normal script or capitals and Akkadian in italics.)

The Akkadian language as attested in the cuneiform texts uses the same four vowels as Sumerian: a, e, i, and u, having probably lost the vowel o under the influence of Sumerian. In addition to the semivowels w and y it uses the following consonants: b, d, g, k, l, m, n, p, q, r, s, t, z, ḫ, ṣ, ś, š, ṭ and the glottal stop ʾ. The Sumerian g̃ is not used in Akkadian but becomes g. The Semitic languages have three h-sounds, h, ẖ and ḫ; Arabic has all three, Hebrew uses only h and ḫ; Akkadian, under the influence of Sumerian, uses only ḫ. Akkadian originally had three sibilants s, ś, and š, but after the Old Akkadian period ś drops out of use. The three emphatic sounds ṣ, ṭ and q, the glottal stop ʾ, and the letter p which are used in Akkadian, do not occur in Sumerian. Thus the Sumerian script was never ideally suited to writing Akkadian. A new sign was invented for ʾ, but otherwise several different conventions were used at different times and in different areas to get over the problems. The distinctions between b and p, between d, t, and ṭ, and between g, k and q are never consistently marked in the script. It is curious that no single agreed solution was ever enforced, such was the strength of the old tradition.

In taking over and adapting the Sumerian syllabary the Akkadian-speaking scribes added to it still further values, increasing the aspects of homophony and polyphony. Thus the Sumerian sign á 'hand' corresponds to Akkadian *idu* 'hand'; hence the sign comes to be used for the syllable *id*, and also for *it*, *iṭ*, *ed*, *et* and *eṭ*. The total number of distinct cuneiform signs in use from the late third millennium onwards is about six hundred, and the number of possible values is far higher. The possible variations did not create as many problems as one might suppose, however, since at any given period and for any given class of text a rather more limited repertoire of signs was used, making life easier both for the scribe and the modern reader. Also in most cases the correct reading of a sign is made clear by the context and by the preceding and following signs.

Although Sumerian had dropped out of common use as a spoken language by the eighteenth century BC and was superseded by Akkadian, it continued to be used by the scribes both as a regular form of shorthand (as in writing udu for *immeru*), in composing many monumental inscriptions (for the sake of tradition), and in copying and recopying Sumerian word-lists and literary texts. By the first millennium for their own convenience the scribes frequently copied Sumerian literature with each Sumerian line followed by its Akkadian translation. The very latest of all cuneiform texts, astronomical texts of the first century AD, are almost entirely written in Sumerian logograms.

The historical divisions
The development of cuneiform during the early Sumerian period has been briefly sketched above. Its further progress is now briefly outlined in order to make the historical terminology intelligible. The accession of Sargon I in 2334 BC marked the beginning of the dynasty of Akkad; the basic language of texts written at this time was Akkadian, specifically the Old Akkadian dialect. With the decline of that dynasty around 2200 BC Akkad was eclipsed and Sumerian became the regular language of administration again, although throughout the next thousand years later kings frequently called themselves kings of Sumer and Akkad. Under the Third Dynasty of Ur (or Ur III) a massive growth of royal bureaucracy occurred which has left us a larger amount of administrative texts than all the other periods of Mesopotamian history put together. Almost every collection of tablets includes Ur III texts.

After the fall of Ur in 2004 BC the dominant dynasties were those of Isin, Larsa and Babylon, in that order. By 1900 BC with the ascendancy of Larsa, Sumerian had again ceased to be the prevalent language and finally gave way permanently to Akkadian. Although the dynasty of Babylon only took control of Sumer and Akkad in 1763 BC in the reign of Hammurapi, the time from 2004 to 1595 BC is commonly known as the Old Babylonian period, and all Akkadian texts of this time are described as Old Babylonian. Texts from the time of the succeeding Kassite Dynasty and the Second Dynasty of Isin are described as Middle Babylonian; this is also the date of the international correspondence found at El-Amarna in Egypt, mostly written in Babylonian, and the archives of Ugarit in Syria. In many respects tablets of the Middle Babylonian period retain a strong similarity in form and script to the earlier ones. The Babylonian texts written in the first millennium BC are quite distinct, but their nomenclature has caused problems. Some scholars describe tablets from 1000 BC to the beginning of the Chaldean (or Neo-Babylonian) Dynasty as Neo-Babylonian, and describe all later tablets as Late Babylonian. Others draw the dividing line after the defeat of the Chaldean Dynasty by Cyrus in 539 BC. There is also a separate literary dialect known as Standard Babylonian which is used in both Babylonia and Assyria.

From the time of Alexander the Great onwards the use of the cuneiform script is increasingly restricted, being superseded by Aramaic; a few legal and literary texts were still written in cuneiform as late as 40 BC, and the last astronomical text is datable to   8

75 AD. The latest texts have a very cursive script and can be extremely difficult to read.

Some of the earliest texts from Assyria are written in Old Babylonian, but a very distinctive group of tablets found at Kanesh (Kultepe) in eastern Turkey proved to be the commercial records of a trading colony from Ashur of the nineteenth century BC. They employ a quite distinctive script and dialect and are identified as Old Assyrian. From the area of Assyria come the fifteenth-century tablets found at Nuzi, but since they show the town to have been controlled by the Hurrian kingdom of Mitanni they are not regarded as Assyrian but are simply described as Nuzi texts. Middle Assyrian texts, mostly from Ashur, begin with the first expansion of Assyria outside its homeland in the thirteenth century BC. The great majority of Assyrian texts, however, belong to the Neo-Assyrian period (1000–609 BC), and come from the royal archives at Nineveh and Kalhu. There is one great advantage in dealing with these texts – they employ a very standardised script. It was fortunate for Assyriologists that these were the first large archives to become available.

The historical development of the cuneiform script which occupies scholars so much today also fascinated the ancient scribes. The collections from Babylon contain many late copies of early historical inscriptions or legal texts made in the seventh or sixth century BC by scribes who had found the originals in temples, private collections or even

Chronological table

Dates (BC)	Sumer/Babylon	Assyria	Elsewhere
3300–2900	Uruk IV–III and Jemdet Nasr periods Brak tablets		Proto-Elamite Susa archives
2900–2600	Early Dynastic I–II period Archaic Ur tablets		
2600–2334	Early Dynastic II–III Enmebaragesi of Kish, c. 2600 Fara tablets Abu Salabikh tablets Ebla archives Girsu (Enannatum I c. 2400) Lugalzagesi of Uruk (2340–2316)		
2334–2154	Dynasty of Akkad Old Akkadian Sargon of Akkad (2334–2279) Naram-Sin (2254–2218) Gudea of Lagash (2141–2122)		Puzur-Inshushinak of Elam
2112–2004	Ur III Dynasty Umma, Puzrish-Dagan and Girsu archives Ur-Nammu (2112–2095) Shulgi (2094–2047)		
2004–1595	Old Babylonian period Archives from Larsa, Nippur, Eshnunna, Sippar, Tell ed-Der, Ur, Kish Sin-kashid of Uruk (c. 1790)	Old Assyrian archives from Kanesh (19th century)	
1894–1595	First Dynasty of Babylon Hammurapi (1792–1750) Samsuiluna (1749–1712)		Mari archives Zimri-Lim (1775–1759)
c. 1550–1155	Kassite Dynasty (Middle Babylonian)		Hittite archives at Boghazkoy (17th–13th century)

8 An astronomical almanac for the year 61/62 AD. BM 40084.

tes (BC)	Sumer/Babylon	Assyria	Elsewhere
		Nuzi archives (15th century)	Mitanni kingdom (c. 1550–1260) Alalakh archives (15th century) (El-Amarna archives (c. 1400)
		Middle Assyrian archives at Ashur (13th century)	Ugarit archives (14th century) Middle Elamite Humban-numena I (c. 1275)
50	Elamite invasion of Babylonia		
57–1026	Second Dynasty of Isin		
000–625	Neo/Babylonian	Neo-Assyrian archives from Ashur, Kalhu, and Nineveh Ashurnasirpal II (883–859) Shalmaneser III (858–824) Sargon II (721–705) Sennacherib (704–681) Esarhaddon (680–669) Ashurbanipal (668–627)	Urartian inscriptions
5–539	Chaldean Dynasty Archives from Babylon Nebuchadnezzar II (604–562) Nabonidus (555–539)		
9–331			Archaemenid Dynasty of Persia Old Persian inscriptions Late Elamite tablets Cyrus (559–530) Darius I (521–486) Xerxes (485–465) Artazerxes III (358–338)
6–323	Alexander the Great		
1	Seleucid Era began Antiochus I Soter (281–260)		
AD	The latest Babylonian tablet		

on rubbish dumps and who had faithfully copied the curious styles of early writing. Among the Neo-Assyrian tablets from Kalhu there is a small group of tablets on which the scribes have drawn archaic signs such as might have been typical of the mid-third millennium BC and annotated them with their modern equivalent, i.e. their Neo-Assyrian equivalent. A century later we find that the archaeologist king Nabonidus, who boasted of finding inscriptions of Hammurapi at Larsa and of excavating for inscriptions of Sargon I and Naram-Sin at Akkad, had some of his own royal bricks and cylinders stamped or inscribed in a script which attempts to imitate the Old Babylonian style.

Numbers

Numbers are found written on cuneiform texts of all types, from the very earliest, before 3000 BC, down to the very latest datable text in AD 75. Over that long time-span the system of writing numbers shows its own development alongside the development of the rest of the cuneiform script.

At all periods the numerical system used by the Sumerians, Babylonians, and those who borrowed from them, is a combination of the decimal system (counting in tens) and a sexagesimal system (counting in sixties). In the earliest periods there are separate symbols for each numerical power:

1	10	60	600 (60×10)	3,600 (60^2)	36,000 ($60^2 \times 10$)

These numbers were written by pressing the larger or smaller ends of a reed stylus into the clay either vertically (to make a circle) or at a slant. When the script becomes truly cuneiform these numbers have a more angular form:

1	10	60	600 (60×10)	3,600 (60^2)	36,000 ($60^2 \times 10$)

In the later Babylonian system (2000 BC to AD 75) for many purposes, especially pure mathematics, numbers were written with a simplified place-value notation whereby the place of a number in a sequence determines its value. There are only vertical and slanting wedges:

1	2	3	4	5	10	20	30	40	50	60	600	60^2	$60^2 \times 10$

The same symbols were also used for writing fractions. So 1 can be 1/60 or $1/60^2$, and so on. Everything depends on the order in which the numbers appear (higher values on the left, lower on the right) and on the context. So:

Υ ⟨ 𝗪𝗪 $60 + 10 + 5 = 75$
or $60^2 + 10 + 5 = 3615$
or even $1 + (15/60) = 1.25$

Π ⟪⟨ 𝗪𝗪 $(2 \times 60) + 40 + 5 = 165$
or $(2 \times 60^2) + (40 \times 60) + 5 = 9605$
or $2 + 45/60 = 2.75$

A small group of signs were also used for simple fractions:

$\frac{1}{2}$ ╫ $\frac{1}{3}$ 𝗨 $\frac{2}{3}$ 𝗝𝗛 $\frac{5}{6}$ 𝗝𝗛

The result could be confusing even for the Babylonians. So, in practice, while the system described was regularly used for pure mathematics and astronomy, in many everyday economic operations numbers and fractions were written out in words (as we may write 100 or one hundred).

Sometimes numbers were also used as a sort of cryptography. Thus the names of some of the major deities could be, and frequently were, written as numbers:

Adad ⟨   Shamash ⟪   Sin ⟪⟨   Ea ⟪⟨   Enlil ⟪⟨⟨

There is a famous case of numerical manipulation in Assyrian history. Sennacherib had sacked Babylon in 689 BC. His son Esarhaddon on succeeding to the throne in 680 BC in a dramatic shift of policy decided to embark on its restoration, and justified it by announcing that whereas the god Marduk had decreed that the city should remain desolate for seventy years he had now relented and turned the number upside down. So seventy became eleven:

70 Υ⟨   11 ⟨Υ

The use of sexagesimal numbers for astronomy by the Babylonians in the last centuries BC gave them a great advantage over contemporary Greek astronomers who had no convenient mathematical notation. As a result many Babylonian astronomical calculations were used by the ancient Greek and medieval Arab astronomers long after knowledge of cuneiform writing was lost. Our present system of counting sixty seconds in a minute, sixty minutes in an hour, and three hundred and sixty degrees in a circle is a survival of Babylonian mathematics.

2
Tablets and Monuments

Tablets and stylus

The overwhelming majority of cuneiform texts were written on clay. Monumental and dedicatory inscriptions can be found on stone, ivory, metal, and glass, and examples have been found of folding ivory writing boards which had a carefully preserved surface of beeswax; but the clay tablet was always the standard writing surface.

Clay was always widely available in Mesopotamia, but would have needed some preparation to ensure that it was of the right quality, at least for writing fine library tablets. Unfortunately the clay from southernmost Iraq has a high percentage of salt which means that some tablets from that area tend to disintegrate in unfavourable atmospheric conditions; but that would not have been a problem for the ancient scribes.

Learning how to make a tablet of the right size and shape with a good, smooth surface for writing on must have been one of the first tasks for trainee scribes. A few experiments show that it is not so easy. The Mesopotamian scribes turned out fine examples at all periods, not just of small single-column tablets but massive eleven-column tablets from the Ur III period measuring over 30 cm square. How they handled them is itself a mystery. One is reminded of the vase painters from Classical Greece who saw fit to record the names of the potters who made the vases; the Mesopotamian scribes might well have done the same, except that so far as we know they made their own tablets. The size of some of these Ur III tablets is probably also the explanation for one regular feature of tablets from that period onwards. The front of the tablet is regularly flat, while the back is convex. Making a tablet perfectly flat on both sides would have been unnecessary; but if the tablet was prepared with at least one side flat then the flat side could be inscribed first, and the tablet could then be lain on its flat face for the reverse to be inscribed without pressure distorting the signs on the front. This characteristic of tablets has often allowed modern scholars to determine which is the front and which the back of some broken fragment of a text.

Most tablets were simply left to dry out after being inscribed. Good quality clay when well dried can be extremely durable, and if not deliberately mishandled will last as long as needed for practical administrative purposes. If necessary it can be moistened again to alter the text. Some tablets, however, being intended for permanent record, whether for legal purposes or as part of a library, were baked. Additionally many of the tablets in museum collections today have been accidentally burnt, since they come from libraries or archives which were destroyed and burnt in antiquity when some foreign conqueror seized a city and sacked it. We owe most of the major collections of tablets to this kind of historical disaster. In the normal course of events unbaked tablets would probably have been re-used eventually as raw material for making new tablets. Where tablets have been baked their colour depends on the temperature to which they have been fired – mostly dark grey or black for tablets destroyed by fire, whitish for tablets baked to an excessive temperature, and a dark orange-brown for tablets baked in modern times under laboratory conditions for their better preservation.

Most tablets are square or rectangular, but not all. Some school texts of the Ur III and Old Babylonian periods, and some land-survey texts of Ur III date, are circular·or bun-shaped. A few tablets prepared for magical purposes are shaped with a wide perforated lug at one end so that they can be specially mounted or threaded through and strung round someone's neck; and others designed for the same purpose are little more than inscribed clay beads. There are also a wide variety of cones, cylinders and prisms, to be discussed later.

These tablets were written with a stylus which was almost always cut from a reed. Its standard Babylonian name is simply *qan ṭuppi*, 'tablet-reed'. Styli in metal or bone were occasionally used, but not by the everyday scribe. Reed of great strength is common in the marshlands of the Near East and its exploitation was itself a large industry. The scribe needed only to take a short piece of reed and trim it to produce a rounded end, a

9 A tablet of the Ur III period; a register of fields. BM 110116.

sharp point, or a flat or sloping end. The manner in which he cut the reed would then affect the style of his writing. From this it is clear that in the third millennium many numbers were written with a round-ended stylus, while the rest of the text was written with a stylus flat at the end. Tablets from the late Old Babylonian period (seventeenth century BC) have a very distinctive slanting script which comes from a stylus with a diagonally cut end, while the Assyrian library texts were written with a flat stylus.

The stylus was not only used to inscribe the text on the tablet. It was also used to mark the lines and columns. From the very earliest periods a cuneiform text was broken up, mostly by natural grammatical or sense units, either into rectangular boxes, or, at least from the Old Akkadian period onwards, into lines separated by rulings. At first the signs were just written in the space between these rulings, but in the Ur III period the practice of using a top line as a guide from which to hang the signs seems to be quite regular; it is still common in the Old Babylonian period, especially for letters and literary texts. Occasionally examples can be found in the Kassite period, but for the most part, rulings in the Kassite and Neo-Babylonian periods separate the lines of text without the signs being hung from them. Some Neo-Babylonian school texts follow the earlier practice, but on literary texts the rulings may run through either the centre or the head of wedges. In general, however, Neo-Babylonian administrative and legal texts are not ruled. The Late Elamite scribes regularly used the side, not the point, of the stylus to make wider rulings, and this appears to be an innovation. The ruling would be made simply by impressing the point of the stylus into the clay and then laying it flat. On a small number of tablets from the royal libraries at Nineveh one can see that the stylus had been replaced by a piece of thread laid across the surface and pressed down.

The rulings made by the stylus marked not only horizontal lines but vertical divisions, or columns of text. Typically a multi-columned tablet would be inscribed first on the left-hand column of the front, or obverse, of the tablet, then on the right-hand column; then the tablet would be turned vertically over its lower edge, and inscribed first on the right column of the reverse and finally on the left column. This curious order harks right back to the days of the earliest pictographic texts. There are some exceptions but they are rare. In general, if a multi-columned tablet does not obey these rules, or if the tablet turns right to left (as the page of a book) then it suggests a forgery.

Very occasionally the stylus is used for some other marks; for instance, a few tablets have ornamental rulings around the outer edge. Some account tablets of the Old Babylonian period listing dozens of individuals have a small check-mark against every tenth person; and a few literary tablets from the Nineveh libraries have a mark against every tenth line, perhaps to give the scribe an easy check on whether he had left a line out. From the Middle Babylonian and Middle Assyrian periods onwards many literary tablets have 'firing holes', which are made by pressing the stylus (or some similar object) right through (or almost through) the tablet from front to back or side to side. It used to be suggested that the purpose of these holes was to help the tablet dry out and stop it from bursting if it was to be baked for better preservation. But consideration of the size of some large Ur III tablets, which could be successfully baked in antiquity without the use of firing holes, suggests that the idea is incorrect. In any case, whatever the reason for their first appearance, they quickly became a matter of tradition. One frequently finds on tablets from the Nineveh libraries that if one copy of a literary text has firing holes other copies of the same text not only have firing holes but have them in the same positions and often disposed in a purely ornamental arrangement. Firing holes are also of interest because close examination of them can show the precise shape of the scribe's stylus.

Occasionally the stylus was used for writing something other than cuneiform. Some tablets of the first millennium BC from Babylonia and Assyria have comments at the end or on the edges in Aramaic; with the gradual decline in use of cuneiform and the rise of Aramaic even in the court of the Assyrian king, remarks in Aramaic would have served as a quick guide to Aramaic-reading filing-clerks. In fact, from a somewhat later period there are also tablets inscribed wholly in Aramaic, and even a small group of tablets from Babylon with Babylonian texts written in the Greek alphabet. Tablets also

10 (*Left*) Neo-Babylonian copy (*c.* 600 BC) of an inscription of Hammurapi (*c.* 1750 BC); the colophon says that the copy was made by the scribe Rimut-Gula from the original text found in the temple Enamtila. BM 46543.

11 (*Right*) A literary tablet with 'firing holes' and a colophon stating that it was written for the royal library of king Ashurbanipal (668–627 BC) at Nineveh. DT 1.

occasionally have inscriptions added in ink or paint, in Egyptian (on a letter from El-Amarna), in Aramaic, or in Assyrian cuneiform.

Other marks were made on tablets by a variety of instruments for different purposes. Many tablets bear the impressions of the seals of witnesses or scribes (discussed below). Others, especially in the first millennium BC, have the impressions of the witness's thumb-nail on the edge, and in such cases the text often says, 'So-and-so has impressed his thumb-nail instead of his seal'. In the Old Babylonian period the same function was performed by impressing the hem of one's garment (*sissiktu*) on the edge of a tablet, though few cases of this have actually been found. Some fabric impressions on tablets may only be the marks of wrapping. Finally, when a tablet had outlived its purpose it could be cancelled by scoring across it with a stylus or some other sharp instrument.

Envelopes

Some tablets, once written, were placed in envelopes of clay, whether for transport, in the case of letters, or for security, in the case of disputed transactions. This practice started in the Ur III period, and was largely restricted to administrative texts. In order to prevent fraud once the record of livestock or materials entering or leaving the royal stores had been written, the tablet was wrapped in a clay envelope; the entire transaction was then re-recorded on the envelope and the responsible supervisor sealed it. In the

12 (*Left*) A Middle Babylonian legal tablet from Alalah, in its envelope. BM 131449.
13 (*Right*) An Old Babylonian letter and its sealed envelope. BM 82199.

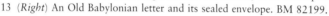

event of a dispute about the quantities involved the envelope could be opened and the record checked. This elaborate precaution prevented anyone from attempting to moisten the clay of the original document and rewrite the numbers. In a few cases envelopes have been opened in modern times and found to contain not a duplicate record of the transaction on the envelope but the original letter authorising the transaction.

In the Old Babylonian period the practice extended to the use of envelopes for legal records, especially sales and disputes over inheritance. These became very elaborate documents, and were sealed by many witnesses in addition to the parties involved. At different periods the seals might either be rolled across the whole width of the envelope or over a space specially left blank, or the text was written on the right-hand side of the envelope and the seals were rolled down the left side or on the left edge. In a curious 12 extension of this practice a group of large legal tablets were prepared and sealed to look as if they were envelopes although they were not.

Envelopes for letters in the Old Babylonian and Old Assyrian period are typically 13 inscribed only with the name of the addressee, 'To my brother, Awil-Adad', or 'To Damqiya and Zikir-Shamash'. The sender normally seals the envelope with his personal seal. Very occasionally he also seals the inner tablet itself for security, and this is specially remarked on in the letter. A few envelopes from the Old Assyrian colony at Kanesh contain both the letter tablet and a small extra piece of clay on which the scribe, who had prepared too small a tablet for the letter, had to continue the message. The fact that literacy was restricted to the professional scribes is emphasised by the opening lines of all these letters, which follow a standard formula: 'Tell Mr A, Mr B sends the following message.' Having been written to dictation by one professional scribe, the letter would be read out to the recipient by another professional scribe.

Although envelopes later than the Old Babylonian period are uncommon, the practice of sending letters in them certainly continued, and examples survive from Neo-Assyrian times. One such, addressed to 'The second officer, my Lord' by Ashur-resua and sealed by him asks, 'Why does my lord refuse to reply to my letter?' To judge by the fact that the present letter still has its envelope, perhaps his lord was simply not opening his mail.

Seals

The practice of sealing tablets and envelopes has already been referred to. In fact seals, 14 either in the form of stamps or cylinders (which would be rolled across the clay), appear 15 long before the invention of writing. The very earliest tablets, which have mathematical 38 notation only, also bear seal impressions. The seals were carved from stone, bone or shell, and the different designs on them served to identify their owners. By the late Early Dynastic period some owners also had their names, or a dedication to a deity, inscribed on their seals. They were at first designed to mark property. When tying up a sack or tying down the cloth cover on a jar the careful Sumerian would squeeze a lump of clay around the knot and seal it; no one could then open the sack or jar without disturbing the seal-impression. Such sealings are known from prehistoric times down to the Old Babylonian period and then again in Neo-Assyrian times. The practice extended to using the seal to record who had authorised or witnessed a transaction, and so many tablets came to be sealed. This usage continued down to the Greek period in Babylonia when we find commercial contracts sealed by small stamp-seals bearing some of the signs of the zodiac as well as thousands of sealings from papyri which have long since decayed.

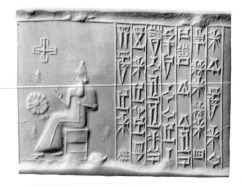

14 (*Left*) An Old Babylonian cylinder-seal. BM 132153.
15 (*Right*) A Kassite cylinder-seal. BM 89128.

Sometimes when the seal bears a personal name, especially a royal name, it can be useful as a means of dating the tablet on which its impression appears; but more often it is the dated and sealed tablets which allow us to study the artistic development of the seals.

As in any other activity anomalies occurred in the use of seals. So in the Old Babylonian period there briefly appear clay seals (known as *burgul* seals) which were one-off creations made for a particular occasion, perhaps because the witness had no personal seal. In Neo-Assyrian records we find that many tablets and clay sealings bear the royal seal of Assyria, depicting the king killing a lion; this would not have been the king's personal seal but a royal household seal. On one tablet of this time from Babylon a scribe making a copy of a royal grant confirming a man's right to temple income has carefully carved a copy of the royal seal in high relief on his tablet, since the royal seal was not available to seal the copy.

Monuments

Kings may have been illiterate, with the exception of Shulgi and Ashurbanipal, but they were well aware of the propaganda value of creating a permanent record of their exploits. They were also concerned to remind the watching gods of how they had cared for their shrines and supported their cults. So besides the everyday receipts and the literary creations we have a separate class of commemorative and dedicatory texts, inscribed at first mostly on stone. Some of the earliest are nothing more than large pebbles, selected simply because stone was more durable than clay, and rarer too in the delta areas of the Tigris and Euphrates.

The earliest such inscription, found on a sherd from an alabaster vase, says only, 'Mebaragesi, king of Kish'. He is to be identified with Enmebaragesi, the father of Akka (the legendary rival of Gilgamesh); the inscription probably dates to *c.* 2600 BC. The vase was prepared for dedication in a temple, and such vases in all varieties of stone continue to be inscribed by the Sumerian and Babylonian kings down to Neo-Babylonian times. More distinctive are the royal statues, mostly rather small but occasionally approaching life-size, as in the case of a famous series of statues of Gudea, ruler of Lagash, *c.* 2130 BC, found at Girsu. The statues are frequently inscribed on the dress or down the back, and until Middle Babylonian times the tradition is preserved of inscribing them in the archaic direction. Over the years almost anything dedicated to a temple could be inscribed with the name of its royal patron, even the agate eyes of the statues of the gods; but some categories of objects became standard vehicles for commemorative inscriptions.

16

16 Statue of Gudea, ruler of Lagash (2141–2122 BC). Courtesy of Metropolitan Museum of Art, New York, Harrison Brisbane Dick Fund, 1959, 59.2.

17 A cone inscription of Ur-Bau, ruler of Lagash (2155–2142 BC). BM 91061.

17   The first category was the clay nail or cone. Decorating the walls of temples with a pattern of small clay nails, sometimes coloured, was a feature of Early Dynastic times, well attested at Uruk. At a later date Sumerian and Old Babylonian legal texts show that it was common for the purchaser of a house to hammer a nail into its wall in the presence of witnesses as a mark of his new ownership. Either the decorative or the legal tradition may lie behind the practice of kings from the time of Enannatum I of Lagash (c. 2400 BC) to Samsuiluna of Babylon (1749–1712 BC) to place inscribed nails, from 5 cm to 25 cm in length, in the walls of temples or chapels, sometimes by the hundred. The inscriptions often give no more than a brief statement, 'Ur-Nammu, king of Ur, who built the temple of Nanna'; but by the Old Babylonian period they have become lengthy recitals of historical and cultic events. In a few cases the inscription records the building of the king's own palace: 'Sin-kashid, the mighty man, king of Uruk, king of Amnanum, has built his royal palace.'

33   The second category was the brick inscription. Almost every building in Mesopotamia was built in brick rather than stone, mostly sun-dried mud brick, but with baked bricks used for the facades of temples and, in particularly prosperous times, even for private houses. From the time of Naram-Sin of Akkad (2254–2218 BC) the kings had their names inscribed or stamped onto at least some of the bricks used to build major public buildings. In view of the number of bricks involved, the scribes' time and effort were saved by preparing a stamp, in clay or wood, on which the inscription was carved in reverse so that it could be conveniently stamped onto hundreds or thousands of bricks in a short space of time. Almost every collection of Near Eastern antiquities has at least one

37 stamped brick of Nebuchadnezzar II (604–562 BC) from the great temple-tower (*ziqqurratu*) at Babylon. The kings of Assyria and Elam were less concerned with such economy of effort and most bricks from these kingdoms are laboriously inscribed along the edges; but this may also reflect their view of the purpose of the inscriptions. When one stamped the surface of a large square brick the inscription would become invisible as soon as it was built into a structure, and only the gods could read it; but if the brick were inscribed along the edge his fellow men too would remember the king's pious works. The inscriptions commemorate royal palaces as well as temples, and in some cases they even commemorate a particular part of a building, such as a well or the pedestal of a statue. A few late bricks have short Aramaic inscriptions, and there are one or two inscriptions in Greek and even in an early form of Arabic.

18   The third category of commemorative inscription was the cylinder or prism. In the

18 (*Left*) A prism inscription
describing the military campaigns
of Sennacherib, king of Assyria
(704–681 BC). H. 15 in (38 cm).
BM 91032.

19 (*Below*) Detail from fig. 18; the
account of Sennacherib's seige
of Jerusalem.

Old Babylonian period a number of prisms were inscribed with lexical lists or literary compositions, but apart from the great cylinders of Gudea (61 cm high, 32 cm diameter) this form was not used for royal inscriptions until Middle Assyrian times. From then on we have some fine examples of six-, eight-, or ten-sided hollow prisms inscribed with lengthy and detailed accounts of the king's military campaigns. (There are particularly fine examples from the reigns of the last great Assyrian kings, Sennacherib, Esarhaddon and Ashurbanipal.) The old idea of recording piety to the gods has been supplemented by the desire to create a permanent historical record, a record which might be updated many times during a king's reign. For most of the Neo-Assyrian kings our knowledge of the political course of their reigns is very largely dependent on an analysis of these prism inscriptions. In spite of the care with which they were prepared, these too were destined to be buried in the foundations of the walls of palaces or temples, much as today we place pennies and copies of newspapers in the foundations of new buildings. In Babylonia the favourite form of such inscriptions was the cylinder, but the cylinders of Nebuchadnezzar II and Nabonidus from Babylon have far less political information and concentrate on details of their temple building and even their own archaeological investigations. The cylinder form survives even in the time of Antiochus I Soter in 281–260 BC.

Most impressive of all were the great inscribed stelae and obelisks of the Assyrian kings, designed to stand out in the open for all to see in the squares and courtyards of the capital cities, depicting the king and describing his conquests. The only early monument comparable to these is the law code of Hammurapi of Babylon, 2.25 m high and inscribed with about 4,000 lines of Babylonian cuneiform. It so impressed the Elamite invaders of Babylonia in 1160 BC that they carried it off to Susa.

On a smaller scale, towns or wealthy private citizens recorded grants of land from the king or exemptions from taxation by preparing stone monuments, on which were carved copies of the original royal decree (written and sealed on a clay tablet) and the symbols of the gods who were invoked as witnesses. These monuments are known as boundary-stones, both from their outward appearance and from the Babylonian term used to describe them (*kudurru*), but almost all of those for which the find-spot is recorded have been found in temples.

3

Scribes and Libraries

Scribal training

Literacy was not widespread in Mesopotamia. The scribes, like any craftsmen, had to undergo training, and having completed their training and become entitled to call themselves dubsar, 'scribe', they were members of a privileged élite who might look with contempt on their fellow citizens. Writing 'Ibni-Marduk dubsar' was the equivalent of writing George Smith, B.A. The scribal profession was under the patronage of the Sumerian goddess Nisaba. Occasionally a scribe would end a long literary text with the comment ᵈnisaba zami, 'Oh Nisaba, praise'. In later times her place was taken by the god Nabu of Borsippa. Whereas other gods were symbolised by animals or stars, his symbol was the stylus.

Our picture of life in Babylonian schools is based on a group of Sumerian literary compositions of the Old Babylonian period. A few of them became part of the standard literary tradition and were still being copied for the library of Ashurbanipal. Schooling began at an early age in the é-dubba, the 'tablet-house'. The headmaster was called ummia (or *ummânu* in Akkadian). He might be assisted by an adda é-dubba, 'father of the tablet-house', and an ugula, 'clerk'. Much of the initial instruction and discipline seems to have been in the hands of a student's 'big brother', an elder student who is pictured as fluctuating between being a friend and a bully. Each of these had to be flattered or bribed with gifts from time to time to avoid a beating.

The French excavations at Mari revealed in the palace of king Zimri-Lim a room with rows of clay benches. This has often been taken as a model of what a Babylonian school would have looked like. Unfortunately no school tablets were found in it so its use cannot be proved. It seems just as likely that students were taught outside in the courtyard, which was the centre of life in any Old Babylonian house. Almost all the private houses of this period excavated at Ur and Isin have a few school texts of one kind or another, suggesting that in wealthy families all the boys were sent to school. At Nippur one part of the town was so full of literary tablets that it has become known to archaeologists as Tablet Hill; it may have been a special scribal quarter.

The first thing the schoolboy had to learn was how to make a tablet and handle a stylus. First steps in writing were made on any piece of clay, learning to impress a simple cuneiform wedge, known in Sumerian as a ge, Babylonian *miḫiṣtu*. The schoolboy practised the horizontal, vertical and sloping wedges over and over again. Then he started on the basic sign-list; but this had to be learnt not only as a series of individual signs but also with the different syllables that they could represent. Thus the sign A stood for á, ya, duru, e and a. He had to learn that A was the basic name of the sign. (He could not write A in capitals, but we do so sometimes to remind ourselves which sign we are dealing with.) Then he would go on to learn what were the many Babylonian equivalents of all these different signs and their alternative values. For instance, one type of sign-list reads di-i DI *di-nu-um* (i.e. the sign DI if read as di is the Sumerian equivalent of *dīnum*, 'lawsuit'); si-li-im DI *ša-la-mu-um* (the sign DI if read as silim is the equivalent of *šalāmum*, 'to be at peace'). After learning the basic signs the pupil had to go on to all the thousands of different Sumerian words that were expressed by more than one sign. Here we can see the continuity of scribal tradition, as the signs being learnt by the very earliest scribes at Uruk were learnt in the same order hundreds of years later by scribes at Abu Salabikh and Uruk, and the Old Babylonian sign-lists were still found in Ashurbanipal's library.

Learning to string signs together to write words seems to have been practised by writing names. That at least is the interpretation of the many small tablets inscribed in a clumsy hand with three or four Sumerian names. Babylonian scribes with few exceptions are remarkably consistent in their application of the cuneiform script to the Sumerian and Akkadian languages. The consonant at the beginning of a syllable is hardly ever linked with a vowel from a preceding syllable; thus the word 'to', Akkadian *ana*, is consistently written *a-na*, not *an-a*. That is a simple enough example, but the principle extends throughout the phonetic representation of the language, and must have been taught in the schools.

At this point the schoolboy was ready to go on to the next stage, which is marked by writing on a different kind of tablet, the round, bun-shaped tablet. On these the teacher would typically write out three lines on one side of the tablet, such as the names of gods, a list of technical terms, a short fragment of literature or a proverb; the schoolboy had to study these carefully, and then turn the tablet over and try to reproduce what the teacher had written. It is usually quite easy to see which side was written by the teacher and which by the schoolboy.

Finally the pupil reached the stage of learning and writing Sumerian literature. Much of Sumerian literature as known in the Old Babylonian period is preserved for us only in school copies. It seems that the boys were copying from dictation, as again and again we find that different copies of a text write the words out slightly differently. That some-

20 An Old Babylonian school tablet inscribed on the front (*left*) by a teacher and on the back (*right*) by a pupil; the text is a Sumerian proverb. BM 104096.

times makes it difficult for us to reconstruct the original form of the text. The literature curriculum was very large and mostly traditional, but even in the Old Babylonian period new compositions were being added, mostly hymns to the gods on behalf of the king.

A separate part of the curriculum was devoted to mathematics, taught by the dubsar nišid, 'scribe of accounting', the dubsar zaga, 'scribe of measurement', and the dubsar ašaga, 'scribe of the field' (i.e. surveyor). In a dialogue between schoolboys the senior boy asks the junior, 'Do you know multiplication, reciprocals, coefficients, balancing of accounts, administrative accounting, how to make all kinds of pay allotments, divide property and delimit shares of fields?' That summarises for us their mathematical curriculum. Museums have dozens if not hundreds of copies of mathematical tables: multiplication tables, tables of reciprocals (for division), of squares and cubes, of square roots and cube roots, and of coefficients. They are the Babylonian equivalent of '60 seconds = 1 minute, 60 minutes = 1 hour, 24 hours = 1 day; 12 inches = 1 foot, 3 feet = 1 yard, 1760 yards = 1 mile', etc., but extended to a wide variety of other purposes such as house-building and tuning musical instruments. There are also compilations of mathematical problems and their solutions designed to teach the students how to apply their knowledge to more or less practical situations, as well as problems in geometry and elementary algebra. The compilations have one curious feature: the numerical answer to all questions on the tablet is the same. If the answer to the first question is six, then so is the answer to the second and third question. This has the advantage that if the student arrives at the answer six then both he and the teacher know that he has correctly understood the necessary procedure. The technical terminology of mathematics is largely Sumerian even though the problem texts are written in Babylonian.

One gets the impression that apart from mathematics the Babylonian scribal education concentrated on Sumerian. One may compare this to the nineteenth-century English public-school tradition that a knowledge of the Greek and Latin languages and literatures and of mathematics were all the education that a man needed. In practice, however, the picture is incomplete. We have copies of Akkadian literary texts, and there is evidence for the more practical side of the curriculum. Just as the modern typist is taught the standard layout for a business letter or a contract, so the Babylonian scribes follow regular patterns in writing such texts, and one can often identify the nature of a tablet from a very small fragment on this basis. A small group of practice letters has a special terminology that marks them out as school letters, and there are similar model contracts. The lexical series, *ana ittišu*, composed in the early Old Babylonian period but surviving only in a few copies from the Late Assyrian libraries, is a collection of Sumerian legal phrases with Babylonian translations, presumably also compiled for use in schools.

The picture given so far relates to the early second millennium BC, since that is the period for which we have the best evidence. As is so often the case, the surviving texts are quite unevenly distributed over time. A small group of copies of Sumerian literary texts of the Kassite period from Nippur shows that the old traditions still survived at that time. The next group of school texts while retaining the spirit of the old tradition have a quite different format. These are texts from Babylonia, and the majority probably come from Babylon itself, dating to the seventh or sixth century BC. They have extracts from more than one composition. Typically they quote two or three consecutive lines from a

21 Assyrian scribes recording booty on one of the campaigns of Tiglath-Pileser III (744–727 BC).
BM 118882.

Sumerian text, giving a translation into Akkadian after each line, then quote from
another part of the same text or from quite a different composition in the same manner,
Sumerian with Akkadian translation, and end with an extract from a lexical text or the
great list of gods known as 'An = *Anum*'. The fundamental change from the early
tradition is the provision of translations of the Sumerian texts. The change is mirrored in
the contemporary libraries, in which Sumerian texts written for permanent record also
have interlinear translations.

21   Of the same late date are the few surviving pictures of scribes, all from the area of
Assyria. The wall paintings at Til Barsip (eighth or seventh century BC) show pairs of
scribes, one writing on a tablet with a stylus, and the other writing on a leather scroll
with a pen, each holding his writing instrument differently. The papyrus was probably
used for writing in Aramaic. Similar pairs of scribes can be seen on the reliefs from the
palaces of Tiglath-Pileser, Sennacherib and Ashurbanipal at Kalhu and Nineveh
(seventh century BC).

Colophons

11   Our knowledge of the scribes is mostly derived from the colophons of tablets. The word
colophon (taken from Greek and meaning 'summit') describes the inscription formerly
placed at the end of a book, containing the title, the printer's name, date and place of
printing, etc. Nowadays books have title pages instead of colophons, but the term is
regularly used by Assyriologists to describe the information which scribes wrote at the

end of tablets. There are three normal constituents to a colophon on a cuneiform tablet, the name of the scribe, the date, and the name of the town in which the tablet was written. Not all tablets have colophons, and some leave out one or another of these elements, but where they do include them all they generally follow this pattern.

Scribes wrote their names on tablets as early as the Fara period (c. 2600 BC). Most of the names have no great significance, but a few are of particular interest. Enheduanna, the daughter of Sargon I, and high priestess of the moongod Nanna at Ur, is one of the few female scribes known from Mesopotamia, and the earliest named author in history; her composition, named after its first line, nin-me-šár-ra, 'Lady of all aspects of life', is a celebration of the goddess Inanna. The next royal scribe is Ashurbanipal, king of Assyria, over 1,600 years later. Although on the whole the literary texts do not record their authorship, a catalogue preserved at Nineveh gives us a list of the authors of some of the best-known compositions such as Sin-liqi-unninni, editor of the Gilgamesh series, and Lu-Nanna, author of the Etana epic. A few texts are attributed to the god Ea or the mythical sage Adapa. Later scribes give not only their own names and the names of their fathers but also the names of an earlier ancestor, the founder of the family or scribal dynasty, and many of these ancestors are identical with the scribes named in the list of authors.

The scribes often describe themeselves simply as dubsar, but sometimes give themselves other titles such as dubsar tur, 'junior scribe' (for instance Nur-Aya who copied out the Old Babylonian 'Flood story' of Atra-hasis), or mašmaššu, 'exorcist'. In a special class was the 'scribe of Enuma Anu Enlil', meaning the scribe of the astrological series entitled 'When the gods Anu and Enlil' – in effect a professional astrologer.

In a few cases even though no scribe's name is recorded we can see that a tablet was written by more than one scribe. A group of circular field-survey tablets of the Ur III period give the dimensions of various fields and the amount of barley that each field was expected to yield at harvest time. On a few tablets the space for the barley yield has been left blank. At first it was suggested that the tablets might only be school texts, but close examination revealed a different explanation. Wherever the barley yield was recorded it had been written in by a different hand, less deeply impressed than the rest of the text, probably when the clay had started to dry out. Apparently the surveyors were only responsible for recording the dimensions of the fields; the yield was worked out separately by the accountants or tax inspectors.

The date on a tablet is the date of writing; in a very few cases we can see that a tablet was written on one day and its envelope on the next day. The dates normally take the sequence month, day, year. The year can be indicated in several ways. In Sumer and in Babylonia of the Old Babylonian period the year was named after an event of some importance occurring either in that year or in the preceding year. The scribes had to keep long lists of such names in order to remember the sequence of documents. The Old Assyrian archives and those from Mari are dated by the name of the limmu, a public official appointed for the year. Again lists of these officials had to be kept. In Kassite times the system of regnal years began, 'The first year of Kurigalzu', and so on, and this system remained standard in Babylonia until the fourth century BC. The Assyrians stuck to the limmu system. Finally in 305 BC a new system was introduced in which all years were numbered in succession from the first year of the Seleucid Dynasty, deemed to be 311 BC.

The place names given in the colophons are particularly useful for the reconstruction of archives which have been distributed through the antiquities trade. But occasionally they can have a different significance. Tablets excavated in one town can have another town's name in the colophon, showing how tablets were carried around the country for business purposes. Or an archaeologist scribe copying an earlier text may describe how he found it 'on the rubbish-tip at Nippur'.

Libraries

The archives in which tablets were stored and found have been referred to many times already. Excavations on almost any town or city site in southern Iraq will turn up at least a few tablets, and if one digs in a town of the Old Babylonian period it seems that one can find a few tablets in almost every house. Small private libraries existed at all periods; recent Belgian excavations at Tell ed-Der revealed a library of some 3,000 tablets in the house of a priest, datable to c. 1635 BC, and the agents of Ashurbanipal reported to him on the contents of several private libraries which they were sending to him from Babylonia. But it is the large state or temple archives that yield the most useful information about the nature of the contemporary economy and administration, and in most periods, with the exception of the Old Babylonian, it is the formal libraries from palace and temple that preserved the mass of literary texts.

The accidents of destruction and recovery have somewhat distorted our picture of the history and development of Mesopotamia. Some periods are extremely well known. The fall of the Ur III empire as a consequence of an Elamite raid in 2004 BC resulted in the accidental burial of huge archives in the ruins of Umma, Puzrish-Dagan and Girsu; only a fraction of the tablets from these sites have been published so far. Similarly the breaking of Babylon's domination of the south by the kings of the new Sealand Dynasty in the time of Samsuiluna (1726 BC) and the collapse of the First Dynasty of Babylon itself with the Hittite raid on Babylon in 1595 BC left large libraries for the archaeologist at Larsa and Sippar. Most famous of all is the library of Ashurbanipal at Nineveh, a priceless source for the reconstruction of Babylonian and Assyrian literature, which comes to us courtesy of the Babylonians and Medes who sacked Nineveh in 612 BC. On the other hand many historical developments are still quite obscure because for long periods we have no significant archives. We have the impression, for instance, that there was a low level of economic activity in Babylonia for a century or two after the end of the First Dynasty of Babylon and again after the end of the Kassite Dynasty; but does the absence of tablets really imply this, or does it only mean that the country was at peace and no one's library was being burnt down?

The great archives from Mari and Ebla have given us a good idea of the nature of a Mesopotamian library, because (for once) they were properly excavated by competent archaeologists who kept a record of what was found in each room and even how the tablets lay on the floor. At Ebla one can see how the library was scattered across the floor as the wooden shelves on which it was stored collapsed. The ancient librarians, like their modern successors, needed systems to record where to find their tablets. In the case of many large tablets from the Ur III period one can see brief notes written on one edge of the tablet, much like the title on the spine of a modern book, written so that the librarian looking along a shelf full of tablets could pick out the one he needed. Mostly this applies to economic texts, but marginal notes are found also, for instance, on tablets containing multiplication tables. Where a library could not afford the expense of wooden shelves tablets were normally stored in jars or baskets, which had an explanatory clay tag tied on. Such tags have been found for baskets of Sumerian literary texts, and matching up the titles recorded on the tags with the titles of known compositions shows us how much is still unknown. The idea of storing tablets in boxes is reflected in literature too: an Old Babylonian epic concerning Naram-Sin begins, 'Open the tablet-box and read the stele'. The scribe wishes to create the illusion that he is telling a story which has been preserved from distant days and lost in some forgotten corner or buried in a box in the foundations of a building.

One device occasionally used, especially in the Old Babylonian period, to ease the burden of storing and manipulating many large tablets was to compile summaries of several contracts on a single tablet. The same thing could apply to literary texts. A recent German excavation at Isin has produced a fragment of a finely inscribed tablet with five different poetic compositions, running to about 7,070 lines in total.

A simple system of keeping track of literary tablets was to add to the colophon a statement of the title of the series to which the tablet belonged and the number of the tablet within that series. So the famous *Epic of Gilgamesh* in its latest version consisted of twelve tablets; the story of the Flood was told on the eleventh tablet. The colophon reads, 'He who saw everything, eleventh tablet'. 'He who saw everything' is the first line of the epic and therefore its title. To ensure that the scribe found correctly the next tablet of the series its first line might also be added to the colophon of the preceding tablet.

The literary libraries largely consisted of standard texts copied and recopied from one generation to the next. Occasional new texts were added from time to time, but they were few by comparison with the great mass of traditional material. Much of this was not what we today would regard as literature, even if Assyriologists continue to call it such. The largest group of texts consists of omens, collections of observations made over hundreds of years concerned with the stars, the appearance of the liver of a sacrificial sheep, the movements of birds, etc. Other categories of texts were the lexical lists, incantations, prayers, and the well-known epic literature. The late Leo Oppenheim, in a summary of traditional Mesopotamian literature, calculated that the whole of the standard corpus as represented in a library like Ashurbanipal's could have run to as many as fifteen hundred different tablets of between eighty and two hundred lines each; for many texts Ashurbanipal had several copies.

Today the discovery of a new library of literary texts generates great excitement among Assyriologists, but such material is not really typical of the production of the Mesopotamian scribes. Most of them, after all their technical training, spent their lives writing lists of deliveries of sheep or issues of barley rations and occasionally taking a letter by dictation. The more successful scribes would end up as senior administrators in the state bureaucracy, but most of their colleagues would have been happy simply with their status as educated men and the knowledge that their training guaranteed them employment.

4

The Geographical Spread

The cuneiform script pioneered by the Sumerians and Babylonians came to be used for some fifteen different languages in its 3,000-year history. Most of these languages used the Sumero-Babylonian signs and syllabary, so the first stage of their decipherment was already done; but the fact that the Sumero-Babylonian system allows several signs to have the same value and each sign to have several values meant that each language in turn required an additional process of analysis and decipherment. A few peoples adopted the idea of writing in cuneiform, but created their own signs which therefore had to be quite separately deciphered (Old Persian, Ugaritic, and related alphabetic scripts). The decipherment of Old Persian and Babylonian is described in the next chapter.

Eblaite

After the pictographic tablets of Tell Brak there is a gap in the record in Syria of several hundred years before the cuneiform script is again found there. Recent Italian excavations at Ebla (Tell Mardikh, near Aleppo) from 1964 onwards have quite transformed the picture of Syria in the mid-second millennium. They revealed a major urban civilisation with widespread trade and commercial contacts and a scribal and literary tradition that had much in common with contemporary Sumer, especially as known from the tablets of Abu Salabikh. Some 10,000 tablets of the Late Early Dynastic period (c. 2500–2400 BC) have been found at Ebla mostly lying on the floor in orderly groups where the wooden shelves of the library had collapsed. Some are only small fragments, but many are huge tablets with 3,000 lines of writing or more.

Much of what is written on these tablets is Sumerian and therefore gives us no clue to the nature of the local language. Thus we can read the Sumerian signs 3 udu-meš and know that they mean both to us and to the scribes of Ebla 'three sheep', but how the scribes of Ebla pronounced what they read is another matter. They had taken over from Sumer the use of clay as a writing medium and Sumerian cuneiform as their script, and for convenience they continued to use the Sumerian signs for most of the objects and transactions that their economic texts had to record. It has been estimated that eighty per cent of the words in the Ebla texts are Sumerian. Interspersed among these Sumerian signs the remaining twenty per cent reflect the local language, now called Eblaite. Broadly speaking most of the nouns, verbs and adjectives occurring in the economic texts are written in Sumerian, and most of the prepositions, pronouns, conjunctions and personal names are written syllabically in Eblaite. The fact that all the basic concepts of the texts are recorded in Sumerian makes it relatively easy to get an idea of their content, but since we have very few texts written entirely in phonetic Eblaite, and these mostly poetic, it is hard to get a good picture of the Eblaite language. It is certainly Semitic, but its exact relation to other Semitic languages such as Akkadian, Amorite and Hebrew is still a matter for academic dispute. The problem is not made any easier by the inadequacies of the Sumerian script for writing a Semitic language, discussed above.

Eighty per cent of the texts are administrative, concerning the textile industry, trade in metals, agriculture and personnel matters. A large group of lexical texts listing Sumerian words for animals, wooden objects, etc., form part of the Mesopotamian tradition of scribal education, and some are directly duplicated by texts found at Fara and Abu Salabikh. Some of them list both the Sumerian term and its Eblaite equivalent; but not all the Sumerian terms are translated, perhaps because they were simply too well known to the Ebla scribes. The few political and geographical texts were, when first found, thought to provide early references to the city of Ashur and to many of the place names of the Bible. But after the first excitement subsided further study has eliminated most of these speculative ideas. Only a few literary texts have been made available so far, Sumerian incantations, a Sumerian hymn to the Lord of Heaven and Earth, and some very problematic texts in Eblaite.

Elamite

The heartland of Elam corresponds very roughly with the area of the modern Iranian oilfields. Although Elamite was one of the three languages of the Persian empire, beside Old Persian and Babylonian, and was therefore inscribed on the various monuments which inspired the first decipherment of cuneiform scripts, including the great rock relief at Behistun, Elamite has long been the poor relation of the three. It is the more curious since, as described in Chapter 1, a native form of pictographic writing (known as Proto-Elamite) appears at Susa almost as early as the earliest texts from Uruk (3100–2700 BC). The nature of the texts suggests a society just as advanced as their Sumerian neighbours. The texts can be partially understood by comparison of the pictograms with parallels from Uruk and by means of mathematical analysis, but they cannot yet be read as a language even though, as at Uruk, the script develops from being purely pictographic to being syllabic.

At the time of the dynasty of Akkad the scribes of Susa had adopted the Sumerian script for commemorative inscriptions, but an Elamite invader, Puzur-Inshushinak, introduced a local variety of linear script based on the Proto-Elamite characters. Although we have a bilingual text inscribed in both Proto-Elamite and Old Akkadian the linear script is still only partly deciphered; it was in any case short lived, and for most of the next six centuries such documents from Elam as survive are written in Sumerian or Babylonian. Only four documents from this period are known to be written in cuneiform in Elamite. It is not until Middle Elamite times from the reign of Humban-numena I (about 1285–1266 BC) onwards that we have inscriptions in the Elamite language again. At this point they use a limited repertoire of signs borrowed from Babylonia to write phonetic Elamite with a few logograms. Most of the texts are on bricks or stone monuments from Susa or nearby Dur-Untash (Choga-Zanbil), but a group of economic texts have been found in American excavations at Tall-i-Malyan.

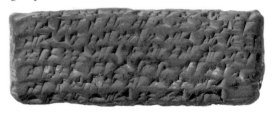

22 A Late Elamite letter, from Nineveh, *c.* 650 BC. Sm 2144.

Although the history of Elamite texts covers more than 2,500 years, the first large group of tablets which can be readily understood is the recently published economic archive of the Achaemenid Persian kings at Persepolis in the fifth century BC. In fact other evidence shows that the Persian court was already using Aramaic for much of its business.

The Elamite language is non-Semitic, and is not directly related to any of the other languages of the Near East. Its decipherment was naturally aided by the availability of the trilingual inscriptions of the Persian kings, but since the available inscriptions cover only a restricted range of subjects our knowledge of the language is still limited, and not more than a dozen scholars are involved in studying it.

Hittite

23   Until the present century the Hittites, who ruled much of present-day Turkey from the seventeenth to the thirteenth century BC, were known only from scattered references in the Old Testament and the histories of the kings of Egypt and Babylonia. They came to light again in 1906 when Dr Hugo Winckler began to excavate their capital city of Hattusas (Boghazköy). In the great palace of the Hittite kings he found a royal archive of 10,000 tablets. Many of these were easily readable in Babylonian, but the large majority were in the previously unknown Hittite language. Fortunately the Hittite scribes used the Babylonian script and a large number of Sumerian or Babylonian words to express Hittite terms – just as the Babylonians had taken over Sumerian terms. When writing historical, legal or ritual texts the scribes would freely alternate between their native Hittite term and its Sumerian or Babylonian equivalent. So a very convenient starting point was provided for deciphering Hittite.

The process of decipherment, begun by the Czech scholar B. Hrozny, was essentially completed by 1933 thanks to the combined efforts of F. Sommer, J. Friedrich, H. Ehelolf and A. Goetze. Hittite belongs to the Indo-European group of languages, although the use of the Sumero-Babylonian syllabary somewhat obscures this fact. Syllables consisting only of vowel + consonant, consonant + vowel, or consonant + vowel + consonant, are not suited to writing groups of more than two consonants, or two consonants at the beginning of a word such as commonly occur in Indo-European languages. It is now agreed that the true name of the language should be Nesite or Nesian (from the Hittite adverb *nešili*) but the name Hittite is now well established by tradition.

The tablets from Hattusas give a good picture of Hittite politics and society. They consist of historical records, international treaties and correspondence, a law code including a table of standard prices, title-deeds for private estates, many religious and magical rituals, and a few mythological stories which have parallels in Greek literature. Historical references to a neighbouring people, the Ahhiyawā, have been seen as early evidence of Homer's Achaeans.

In addition to Hittite two other closely related Indo-European languages were spoken in the Hittite kingdom, Palaic and Luwian. A small number of texts in these two languages have been found in the archives at Hattusas, together with short passages in the pre-Hittite language Hattian. All three languages are written in the Hittite cuneiform script.

Hurrian

This is the language of the Hurrian peoples who appear in the Near East at the end of the third millennium BC in the area of the upper Euphrates in north Syria and survive there

23 A bilingual tablet written in Hittite and Luvian; a ritual against plague. BM 108548.

until *c.* 1000 BC. About 1500 BC they set up the independent kingdom of Mitanni. The first known reference to this kingdom appeared in a letter from Amenophis III (1417–1379 BC) of Egypt to their king Tushratta. It was found in a large archive of international correspondence at El-Amarna in Egypt in 1887 and is still the most important single source of information about their language. A number of texts in Hurrian have been found in the Hittite archives from Hattusas (*c.* 1400 BC), where passages in Hurrian are introduced by the word *ḫurlili*, at Mari (*c.* 1750 BC) and at Ugarit (*c.* 1500 BC). The texts from Ugarit are written in a consonantal script and include a Sumero-Hurrian vocabulary, and there are fragments of a Hurrian translation of the Babylonian *Epic of Gilgamesh* from Hattusas. Hurrian names and terminology also appear in a wide variety of texts throughout the cuneiform milieu in the mid-second millennium BC. Hurrian is an ancestor of the Urartian language, but otherwise its relation to other languages is quite obscure; modern scholars have often named it Mitannian.

The Hurrians are of particular historical interest as the people who introduced the horse and chariot warfare to the Near East. A treatise on horse-training by Kikkuli of Mitanni found at Hattusas includes a number of technical terms in yet another language, which seem to have Sanskrit elements; it is not otherwise known and no satisfactory name has yet been found for it.

Urartian

The Urartians appear in history as the northern neighbours and rivals of the Assyrians from the thirteenth to the seventh centuries BC. They took over from them both the cuneiform syllabary and the Assyrian sign forms, but their own language was related to Hurrian. Since the Urartian homeland lay around Lake Van, A. H. Sayce, who published the first lengthy study of the language in 1882, called it Vannic. The chief deity in Urartu was the god Haldi, so others have called the language Haldian or Chaldian, but today the name Urartian is agreed on.

Such Urartian inscriptions as survive are mostly written on stone monuments and are the historical records of the kings of Urartu. Some texts are found inscribed on helmets, shields and metal vessels, naming their owners or donors, and there are about thirty clay tablets recording economic transactions. Already in 1826 E. Schulz copied forty-two cuneiform inscriptions in the area of Lake Van, but after he was murdered by a Kurdish chief in 1829 his copies were not published until 1840. Already by 1848 the Irish scholar Edward Hincks had taken the first steps towards the decipherment of Urartian, and this even before the decipherment of Babylonian and Assyrian had made much progress. The work of decipherment was continued by F. Lenormant and A. D. Mordtmann and was essentially completed with Sayce's publication (though, as with any newly deciphered language, vast progress has been made since his day). Since the Urartian kingdom extended over the Caucasus mountains much of the basic research into Urartian language and archaeology is being done by Soviet scholars.

Ugaritic

24   In 1929 French excavations at Ugarit (Ras Shamra) on the Syrian coast produced a quite unexpected new variety of cuneiform script datable to the fourteenth century BC. Unlike the Sumero-Babylonian form this one had only thirty signs (and a vertical word divider)

24 Part of the Ugaritic epic of Aqhat.
Musée du Louvre, Paris.

and was plainly alphabetic. Remarkably the script was deciphered within a year by the independent efforts of H. Bauer, E. Dhorme and C. Virolleaud. The language proved to be related to Hebrew, and the mythological texts found at Ugarit concerning the god Baal and his entourage have been a fruitful source of material for scholars seeking early parallels to the poetic texts of the Hebrew Bible. In practice economic documents in both Ugaritic and Babylonian were also found at Ugarit, but it is the mythological texts

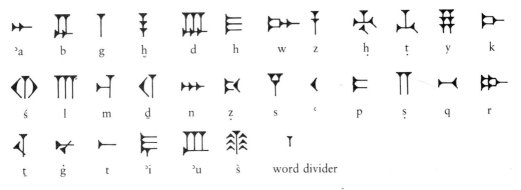

25 The Ugaritic alphabet.

which have stolen the limelight. There are over 1,000 tablets altogether written in Ugaritic, and the order of the alphabet is known from some tablets on which teachers or students wrote their ABC. It is almost identical with the traditional order of the Hebrew and Phoenician alphabets, and it is now apparent that it was the existence of contemporary linear alphabetic scripts that inspired the invention of the Ugaritic system. The full alphabet of thirty signs was only used in administrative texts. In the literary texts the scribes used a shorter alphabet, leaving out the last three signs.

It was probably the local use of the Ugaritic script that inspired a shorter cuneiform alphabet in Cyprus, Syria, Lebanon and Palestine. It is based on the Ugaritic script but has only twenty-two signs. Unfortunately very few such texts have been found so far, so we are unable to determine which of the local Semitic languages or dialects was being written in each case. The relevant texts have been conveniently assembled in a recent publication by É. Puech.

Old Persian

This cuneiform script was the first to be deciphered. In retrospect this is a remarkable fact since the normal requirement for the decipherment of a script is the availability of a large body of text to work on, and by comparison with Babylonian and Sumerian the amount and variety of Old Persian texts are very limited. However, at the time they were both more accessible and more legible than the other varieties of cuneiform. All of these points are in fact the result of the circumstances of the script's invention.

It has recently been suggested that the Old Persian script was invented on the instructions of the Achaemenid Persian king, Darius I (521–486 BC), in order to give him a distinctive script, comparable to those used by the kings of Babylon and Assyria, with which to inscribe his royal monuments. Even the cuneiform inscription on the tomb of Cyrus (559–530 BC) is now thought to have been placed there on the orders of Darius I. The script is found on rock reliefs, the stonework of the Achaemenid buildings at Pasargadae and Persepolis, gold, silver and stone commemorative tablets, and a number of seals and calcite vases, but on very few clay tablets. For everyday purposes the Persian court and administration used either Elamite cuneiform or Aramaic, and the use of Old Persian was entirely abandoned after the time of Artaxerxes III (358–338 BC). Darius's inscription on the rock at Behistun, which was used by Rawlinson to complete Grotefend's decipherment of the script, remains the longest of all texts in Old Persian.

The script has thirty-six characters. Apart from three vowels (a, i, u) all are syllables consisting of a consonant and one of the three vowels. In addition a single slanting wedge is used as a word divider, and there are five separate ideograms for 'king', 'country', 'earth', 'god', and Ahuramazda (the name of the Persian deity), and numerical symbols. There are variant forms of the word divider and the ideograms for country and Ahuramazda. Some Old Persian texts are given in Chapter 5. In the accompanying table the conventions used by R. G. Kent have been followed: x represents Scottish ch as in loch, c represents English ch as in church, θ represents English th as in thin, ś represents a hard s, š represents English sh.

In addition to the languages discussed above a number of languages not normally written in cuneiform are represented by personal names or technical terms appearing in cuneiform texts. For instance in the Ur III and Old Babylonian period a large population of Amorites migrated into Mesopotamia and exercised considerable political influence. Almost all the kings of the Old Babylonian Dynasty bear Amorite names, and all that we know of this Semitic language is derived from the study of these names. The Kassite language is also known only from personal names and from two Babylonian tablets which are dictionaries for translating Kassite names. Similarly in the first millennium B C many Egyptian, Greek, Arab, Jewish and Iranian names appear in the Late Babylonian economic texts.

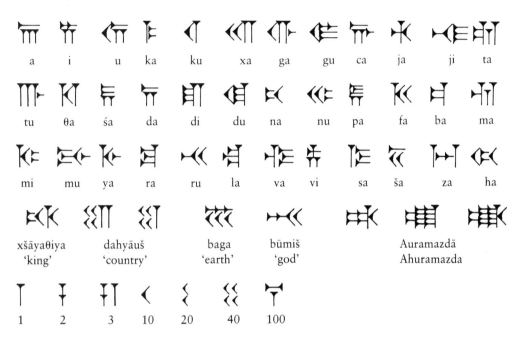

a	i	u	ka	ku	xa	ga	gu	ca	ja	ji	ta

tu	θa	śa	da	di	du	na	nu	pa	fa	ba	ma

mi	mu	ya	ra	ru	la	va	vi	sa	ša	za	ha

xšāyaθiya 'king'	dahyāuš 'country'	baga 'earth'	būmiš 'god'	Auramazdā Ahuramazda

1	2	3	10	20	40	100

26 The Old Persian script.

5

Decipherment

The story of the decipherment of cuneiform starts in the eighteenth century with travellers visiting the ruins of Persepolis, the capital city of the Achaemenid Dynasty of Persia (559–331 BC). There they found and copied a number of short inscriptions from the doorways of the palaces, each of which was written out in three different forms of cuneiform script. In the eighteenth century the identity of the site was unknown, but study of the Greek histories eventually led people to believe that it was indeed Persepolis, and that its construction might have been the work of the Persian kings famous from the histories of Herodotus – Cyrus, Darius and Xerxes.

The time of the Achaemenid Dynasty saw the rise to prominence of the Zoroastrian religion and the worship of its supreme god Ahuramazda. The sacred literature of the Zoroastrians, the so-called Zend-Avesta, had fortunately become known to European scholars from the publication of its text by A. Duperron in 1771, and knowledge of the Avestan language and the related Pahlavi texts which were published about the same time was to give many clues to the decipherment of the Old Persian cuneiform script.

The first success in deciphering Old Persian was achieved by the German G. F. Grotefend. It had already been seen that the simplest version of each text used only a limited number of signs, and was therefore probably written in an alphabetic script. It had also been suggested that the single slanting wedges represented word dividers. Examination of the texts suggested that the script was written from left to right: for instance the sign group which we now transliterate as xa-ša-a-ya-θa-i-ya appears in fig. 28 at the ends of lines 1 and 3 complete, but also broken into two parts at the end of line 2 and the beginning of line 3. The texts illustrated here in figs 27 and 28 were both known to Grotefend. On the basis of the recently translated Pahlavi texts Grotefend guessed that this sign group (xa-ša-a-ya-θa-i-ya) would be the word for king, and that in lines 2–3 its repetition meant 'king of kings'. So the text of fig. 28 probably said, 'A, king . . ., king of kings'. The king's name at the beginning of fig. 28, line 1, appears again in line 3 of fig. 27, followed again by xa-ša-a-ya-θa-i-ya. So he presumed that in this inscription King B was describing himself as son of King A. Grotefend suspected that the texts might concern the kings Darius and his son Xerxes, so using forms for these two names which he derived from Greek, Hebrew and Avestan he suggested reading the signs as follows:

27
28

| d | a | r | h | e | u | sh | | kh | sh | h | e | r | sh | e |

Three signs, e, r and sh, seemed to be the same in the two names.

He then tackled the word for king (which we have transliterated as xa-ša-a-ya-θa-i-ya in the light of modern knowledge). The values already arrived at gave him:

《𒀭 𒀭 𒀭 𒀭 𒀭 𒀭 𒀭

kh   sh   e   h   ?   ?   h

In Duperron's edition of the Avesta he found the royal title khscheio. This he took as confirmation that the language of the cuneiform inscriptions was Avestan, and he assigned the values i and o to the two previously unidentified characters. Looking for the name of Darius's father, Hystaspes, in the first inscription he fitted it to the signs which we now transliterate as vi-i-ša-ta-a-sa-pa:

𒀭 𒀭 𒀭 𒀭 𒀭 𒀭 𒀭

g   o   sh   t   a   s   p

The signs o, sh and a were in the right places and he now had the signs for g, t, s, and p.

This much he had already achieved by 1802. Comparing his results with the modern transcriptions one can see that the values of some signs were incorrect, and that he had not yet discovered that the script was not fully alphabetic, since in many cases the consonants have a specific vowel linked to them. Still it was a start, and a slow process of comparing various inscriptions with names known from historical sources gradually yielded approximate values for other signs.

The next big step forward was taken by the Englishman Henry Rawlinson, who began in 1835 the lengthy process of copying the huge inscriptions of Darius carved on the side of a mountain at Behistun in western Iran. Rawlinson had already managed to reach the same kind of results as Grotefend on the basis of the triple texts of two inscriptions found at Mount Elwend, but he saw the need for lengthy texts of varied content to give a better chance of thoroughly understanding the language being deciphered.

The texts carved for Darius at Behistun commemorated his victories in establishing his rule over the Persian Empire, and were accompanied by a relief depicting Darius and some of the kings whom he took captive. Like the shorter inscriptions already known, Darius's inscriptions were in three languages, now identifiable as Old Persian, Elamite and Babylonian. The task of copying the Old Persian text (414 lines in all) was completed little by little over some ten years, since the texts were inscribed on a steep cliff, needing all Rawlinson's skill and daring as a climber to reach them. It was well worth the effort, since the complete text and the many shorter captions contained the names of all the peoples of Darius's empire, and comparison with the Greek histories allowed Rawlinson correctly to identify many more cuneiform signs. Armed with these and his knowledge of Avestan and Sanskrit Rawlinson was able to go on to produce a complete translation of the whole text in 1846. Other scholars, notably Edward Hincks in Ireland, had made significant contributions to the progress of decipherment, but it was Rawlinson's work at Behistun which set the seal on the whole enterprise.

Continued on p. 52

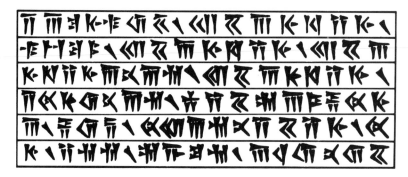

27 Old Persian: carved above the figure of Xerxes in the doorways of his palace at Persepolis.

xa-ša-ya-a-ra-ša-a : xa-ša-a-ya-θa-i-ya : va-za-ra-
ka : xa-ša-a-ya-θa-i-ya : xa-ša-a-ya-θa-i-ya-a-
na-a-ma : da-a-ra-ya-va-ha-u-ša : xa-ša-a-ya-θa-
i-ya-ha-ya-a : pa-u-ša : ha-xa-a-ma-na-i-ša-i-ya

Xšayârša xšâyaθiya vazraka xšâyaθiya xšâyaθiyânâm Dârayavahauš xšâyaθiyahyâ puśa
Haxâmanišiya
Xerxes, the great king, the king of kings, the son of Darius the king, an Achaemenian.

28 Old Persian: carved above the figure of Darius in the doorways of his palace at Persepolis.

da-a-ra-ya-va-u-ša : xa-ša-a-ya-θa-i-ya :
va-za-ra-ka : xa-ša-a-ya-θa-i-ya : xa-ša-a-
ya-θa-i-ya-a-na-a-ma : xa-ša-a-ya-θa-i-ya :
da-ha-ya-u-na-a-ma : vi-i-ša-ta-a-sa-pa-ha-ya-
a : pa-u-śa : ha-xa-a-ma-na-i-ša-i-ya : ha-
ya : i-ma-ma : ta-ca-ra-ma : a-ku-u-na-u-ša

Dârayavauš xšâyaθiya vazraka xšâyaθiya xšâyaθiyânâm xšâyaθiya dahyunâm Vištâs-
pahyâ puśa Haxâmanišiya hya imam tacaram akunauš
Darius, the great king, king of kings, king of countries, son of Hystaspes, an
Achaemenian, who built this palace.

Once the meaning of the Old Persian texts had been established the Elamite and Babylonian texts had to be tackled. The Behistun texts in these languages were copied by Rawlinson in 1844 and 1847, with even greater difficulty than he had faced when copying the Old Persian texts. The Elamite texts of the Achaemenid period use 123 different signs, so the texts were clearly written syllabically, not alphabetically. Again the values of the different signs were established by comparing the writing of names in the Elamite and Old Persian texts. This would not always have been easy – compare the various writings of Hystaspes in figs 28–30: Old Persian vi-i-ša-ta-a-sa-pa-ha-ya-a, El-amite ¹mi-iš-da-áš-ba, Babylonian ¹uš-ta-as-pa. Since the Elamite language was not related to any other known language there was not the help available which Avestan and Sanskrit had provided for Old Persian, but by 1855 Edwin Norris, to whom Rawlinson had given his notebooks, had arrived at the correct decipherment of most of the script. Rawlinson and Hincks meanwhile concentrated on the Babylonian texts, which were the more interesting since they could be related to the stray texts in Babylonian and Assyrian which had been found in Mesopotamia in the preceding decades and to the flood of texts which were now coming from Layard's excavations at Kalhu (Nimrud).

The Babylonian texts were altogether more difficult in some respects, since, as fig. 30 shows, they were not written entirely phonetically but used a number of 'logograms' (signs each standing for a word). Thus in fig. 30 LUGAL is the Sumerian sign for king, and is used in place of the Babylonian word šarru (in its various forms); KUR is Sumerian for Babylonian mātu, land, and in this case plurality is expressed by doubling the sign KUR and adding the Sumerian plural sign MEŠ. In the case of GAL-ú, the Sumerian GAL has a phonetic complement ú to indicate that the signs are to be read as rabû. None of this was at first apparent to the decipherers, who found themselves confronted by a far larger and more confusing set of signs than had been the case with Old Persian and Elamite (over 600 signs are in use in Babylonian and Assyrian in the first millennium BC). However, the decipherers, Rawlinson, Hincks and Jules Oppert, had an advantage in that it was supposed that the Babylonian language (which they assumed was hidden in this script) would be related to Hebrew and Aramaic and other languages of the Semitic group. The Semitic languages as then known were typically written out without regular indication of the vowels in a word. So when Rawlinson came across the different signs for ba, bi, bu, ab, ib, ub he would at first have regarded them all as different ways of writing b, and only later did he realise that the signs were significantly different and included the vowels which would contribute much to the understanding of Babylonian grammar.

In the case of the decipherment of Babylonian the tortuous path by which Rawlinson and his competitors arrived at their goal is only partly hinted at in his notebooks, now preserved in the British Library. It was a path which often reduced him to despair, and in old age he was himself quite unable to account for how he had achieved success. International argument has returned frequently to the question of how much of the credit for success is due to Rawlinson himself. There is no doubt that Hincks in particular made significant contributions for which he has been given little credit. But the fact remains that the first major landmark was Rawlinson's publication of the cuneiform text, transliteration and translation of the Babylonian inscription from Behistun in 1851. Even then the varied nature of Babylonian cuneiform, its contemporary equivalent in Assyria, and its predecessor in Sumer, was only partially apparent, and in some senses the decipherment of this branch of the cuneiform scripts continues to this day.

6

Sample Texts

Assyriologists habitually write out Sumerian in lower case Roman script and Akkadian in italics. But for texts of the first millennium words taken over from Sumerian are written in Roman capitals. There is no good reason for the difference; it is merely arbitrary.

š represents sh; ṣ and ṭ are emphatic consonants; ḫ is a hard h.
ā ē ī ū are long vowels.
Accents and subscript numbers are used to distinguish cuneiform signs which have the same sound, e.g. ša, šá, šà, ša₄.
[1,d] and [ki] are the cuneiform markers for personal names, divine names and towns. GIŠ and URU are markers for wooden objects and towns. Writing [ki] rather than KI, etc., is again only an Assyriological convention.

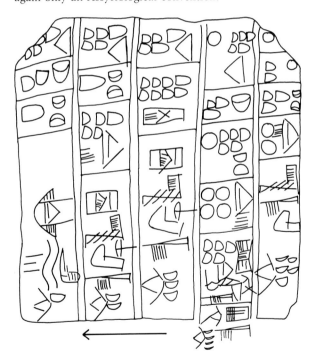

31 A tablet of the Jemdet Nasr period. BM 116730. (See also front cover.)
The tablet is shown oriented in the late direction. However confusing this may be, scholars persist in exhibiting and publishing the early texts as if they had been written

and read in the late manner. To see the tablet as an early Sumerian scribe would have read it, turn this page so that the arrow points upwards, not sideways. Turning the page back to its natural direction the horizontal lines of the tablet have become vertical columns. Compare fig. 7, in which the little squares have expanded into lines.

This text cannot yet be fully translated, but it illustrates the general character of the early texts. Each column concerns the issue of commodities as rations for a particular day. The day number is given at the bottom of the column, 'day 1', 'day 2', 'day 3', ('day 4' is out of sight on the bottom edge), 'day 5'. Five different commodities are being issued; we shall call them A, B, C, D and E.

day   A   B   C   D   E

On day 1 they issue 5 A, 1½ B, 1 C; on day 2, 5 A, 1 C, 5 D; on day 3, 5 A, 8 E; on day 4, 15 A, 3 B, 15 C, 40 D; on day 5, 10 A, 2 B, 3 C, 20 D. The various commodities are summarised on the reverse of the tablet. On day 4 there is also an issue of 5 items of another commodity identified by a lengthy group of signs. The remaining signs at the end of each column are not yet understood.

32 A tablet of the Fara period; Sumerian. BM 15833.
Like the previous tablet this one would probably have been read in antiquity from a different angle. It is a list of cattle being received from or distributed to various temple herds. The signs are still grouped in boxes; in a later text 'from Enlil' would be written ki ᵈen-líl

1 še gu₄	1 barley-fed ox	3 ᵈen	3 from the god Enlil
6 ú gu₄	6 grass-fed oxen	ki líl	
ᵈšuruppak	the god Shuruppak	2 gu₄	2 oxen
3 še gu₄	3 barley-fed oxen	6 ú gu₄	6 grass-fed oxen
6 ú gu₄	6 grass-fed oxen	kin nir	Mr Kinnir
ᵈgi	the god Gibil	7 gu₄	7 oxen
bil		ki ᵈen zu	from the god Suen

33 A brick inscription of Ur-Nammu, king of Ur (2112–2095 BC); Sumerian. BM 90015.
ᵈinanna nin-a-ni ur-ᵈnammu nita-kala-ga lugal-uriᵏⁱ-ma lugal-ki-en-gi-ki-uri-ke₄ é-a-ni
mu-na-dù
For Inanna his lady Ur-Nammu, the mighty man, king of Ur, king of Sumer and Akkad,
has built her temple.

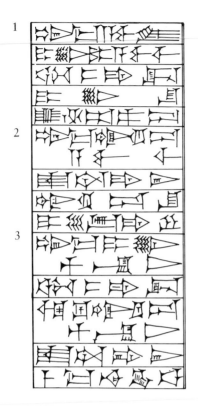

34 Part of the code of laws of Hammurapi, king of Babylon (1792–1750 BC); Babylonian.

1. *šum-ma a-wi-lum i-in* dumu *a-wi-lim úḫ-tap-pí-id i-in-šu ú-ḫa-ap-pa-du*
šumma awīlum īn mār awīlim uḫtappid īnšu uḫappadū
If a man destroys the eye of another man, they will destroy his eye.

2. *šum-ma* gìr-pad-du *a-wi-lim iš-te-bi-ir* gìr-pad-du-*šu i-še-eb-bi-ru*
šumma eṣmet awīlim ištebir eṣmetšu išebbirū
If he breaks the bone of another man, they will break his bone.

3. *šum-ma i-in* maš-en-kak *úḫ-tap-pí-id ù lu* gìr-pad-du maš-en-kak *iš-te-bi-ir* 1 ma-na
kù-babbar *i-ša-qal*
šumma īn muškēnim uḫtappid ū lū eṣmet muškēnim ištebir 1 mana kaspam išaqqal
If he destroys the eye of a subordinate or breaks the bone of a subordinate he shall pay
one mina of silver.

35 The inscription above a picture of Sennacherib, king of Assyria, at the seige of
Lachish. Assyrian.

1. ¹ᵈsin-PAP.MEŠ-SU šar₄ ŠÚ šar₄ KUR aš-šur
   Sin-aḫḫē-erība šar kiššati šar māt aššur
   Sennacherib, king of the world, king of Assyria

2. ina GIŠ.GU.ZA ni-me-di ú-šib-ma
   ina kussī nēmedi ūšibma
   sat on a throne and

3. šal-la-at URU la-ki-su
   šallat Lakisu
   the booty of Lachish

4. ma-ḫa-ar-šu e-ti-iq
   maḫaršu ētiq
   passed before him.

36 Alternative writings of the names of some Assyrian kings.

Ashurnasirpal, Aššur-nasir-apli – ¹AŠ-PAP-A, ¹aš-šur-PAP-A

Shalmaneser, Šulmānu-ašared – ¹ᵈšul-ma-nu-MAŚ

Sargon II, Šarru-kīn – ¹šárru-GIN, ¹LUGAL-GI.NA

Sennacherib, Sin-aḫḫē-erība – ¹ᵈsin-PAP.MEŠ-eri₄-ba, ¹ᵈEN.ZU-ŠEŠ.MEŠ-SU

Esarhaddon, Aššur-aḫ-iddina – ¹AŠ-PAP-AŠ, ¹ᵈaš-šur-PAP-AŠ

Ashurbanipal, Aššur-bāni-apli – ¹aš-šur-DÙ-A, ¹ᵈAN.ŠÁR-DÙ-A

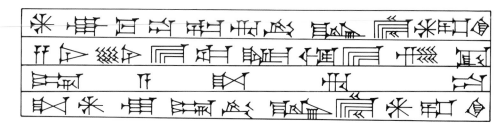

**37 A brick inscription of Nebuchadnezzar II, king of Babylon (604–562 BC);
Babylonian.**

1. ^d*nabu-ku-du-úr-ri-uṣur* LUGAL KÁ.DINGIR.RA^{ki}
 Nabû-kudurri-uṣur šar Babili
 Nebuchadnezzar, king of Babylon,

2. *za-ni-in é-sag-íl ù é-zi-da*
 zānin Esgila u Ezida
 patron of Esagila and Ezida,

3. IBILA *a-ša-re-du*
 aplu ašarēdu
 eldest son

4. *ša* ^d*nabu*-IBILA-URÙ LUGAL KÁ.DINGIR.RA^{ki}
 ša Nabû-apla-uṣur šar Babili
 of Nabopolassar, king of Babylon.

7

Fakes

Any form of document can became a subject for the collector, and cuneiform documents are no exception. Whether one seeks examples of calligraphy, literature, postal history, or merely curios, a cuneiform tablet can be an attractive item. Vast quantities of tablets were brought to Europe and North America between 1890 and the early 1930s and found their way into private collections and local museums. Along with the genuine tablets came many fakes, and both continue to circulate as collections are formed and dispersed. The difficulties of the cuneiform script mean that an experienced Assyriologist has little problem in recognising a fake except in the case of really well-made casts. However, few museums and even fewer dealers have any expertise in cuneiform, and most have to rely heavily on advice from a small number of scholars. Some comments on the subject of cuneiform fakes may therefore be interesting and helpful both to potential collectors and to museum visitors.

Whenever someone starts to collect, and especially when he is prepared to pay good money for objects, someone else sees an opportunity to make an easy profit by supplying the new market with forgeries. So the first cuneiform forgeries of modern times appear already in the 1820s, in the collections of C. J. Rich, British Resident in Baghdad. His manuscript collection contains a number of faked tablets and cylinder inscriptions of Nebuchadnezzar II moulded in the local clay from originals found at Babylon. No doubt these were the product of the local merchants of the nearby town of Hillah. Since the decipherment of cuneiform still lay in the future it would not have been too easy to detect the forgeries, but it is suggestive that none of them are illustrated in the beautiful drawings of Rich's cuneiform collection made by Carl Bellino.

Later in the nineteenth century casts of tablets appear in larger numbers, and with some of these one encounters a special problem, as they were made by two of the most professional people in their field, the Ready brothers. They were not in fact made as fakes at all, but as bona fide replicas, and as such have occasionally caused problems for later museum curators. The Ready brothers were employed to make official copies of many works of art for the British Museum, and had access to numerous very well preserved cuneiform tablets on which to try their skill; some of the resulting casts have even caused confusion within the Museum.

The first warning of a cast of a tablet is its weight; a plaster cast tends to be noticeably lighter than a clay tablet of similar size. The second indication is the mark around the edge of the cast where the two pieces of the cast, front and back, have been fitted together. Occasionally the truth also appears from the direction in which the tablet turns. When reading a book we turn the pages from right to left; but cuneiform tablets were turned bottom to top. Only a handful of genuine tablets break this rule. So if a tablet appears to turn right to left it is almost certainly a forgery.

A very simple warning is carried by a large number of fakes made in Turkey in the early years of this century – a slip of Turkish newspaper pasted on to one edge. It is remarkable how many tablets still circulate in the market today with this forger's trademark surviving so visibly.

Another danger sign is the nature of the inscribed object itself. The vast majority of inscriptions written in antiquity were written on clay. Inscribed seals are much less common, although very durable, but are quite often faked simply because they are so much prized by collectors. But inscribed statues surviving from antiquity, especially complete statues, are very rare. Despite that there is nowadays a flourishing trade in the Levant in crude statues made in some easily worked stone brazenly carrying on the front or back large cuneiform inscriptions which immediately proclaim them forgeries. On the whole forged inscriptions on metal vessels and weapons seem to be incised by a rather more competent group of craftsmen. With all objects other than clay tablets there is the added difficulty that many items were also made in antiquity by second-rate craftsmen. A wealthy Babylonian bureaucrat could well afford a perfectly cut cylinder seal from the best seal-cutter in town while a small-time merchant in north Syria might carry a seal of very indifferent workmanship cut by a man who had only a slight knowledge of cuneiform. Even experienced curators often find it hard to tell the difference between third-rate antiquities and fakes.

The easiest test of authenticity is to take a long hard look at the cuneiform inscription itself. As explained before, from the later third millennium onwards cuneiform signs are almost exclusively created from three different types of wedges, vertical wedges having the head at the top, horizontal wedges with the head at the left, and slanting wedges with the head either in a central position or at the upper left end. The forger frequently ignores this rule. So any inscription where individual wedges point upwards, to the left, or slant up to the right, should be treated with suspicion. Excessive repetition of a small group of signs is also a common hallmark of an unimaginative forger.

Ultimately the best defence against fakes is to acquire some visual familiarity with the genuine article, whether by frequent visits to those few museums that display cuneiform inscriptions, or by building up a library of photographs. One should bear in mind that although some tablets are masterpieces of calligraphy, the vast majority of inscriptions were written by ordinary scribes for purely practical or commercial use, and that these are the texts that one will most commonly find in local museums or private collections.

38 An Old Babylonian cylinder-seal. BM 103314.

Where to see Cuneiform Inscriptions

The following is a summary of the principal collections of cuneiform inscriptions. It includes some quite small collections which hold material from particular sites or have published catalogues. Many collections have been built up entirely from purchases on the antiquities market. Others are largely the result of sponsoring excavations; these are briefly summarised. The references to excavations will give some idea of the history of archaeological exploration, especially in Iraq. On many sites excavation has continued to the present day.

Belgium
Brussels, Musées Royaux d'Art et d'Histoire.

Canada
Toronto, Royal Ontario Museum.

Denmark
Copenhagen, The National Museum.

Eire
Dublin, The Chester Beatty Library and Gallery of Oriental Art.

France
Paris, Musée du Louvre – tablets from excavations at Girsu (1877–1933), Susa (1884–1978, Mari (1933–), Ugarit (1929–), etc.
Paris, Collège de France.
Paris, Ecole pratique des Hautes Etudes, IVe Section.
Strasbourg, Bibliothèque Nationale et Universitaire.

Germany
Berlin, Staatliche Museen, Vorderasiatisches Museum – tablets from excavations at Babylon (1899–1917), Fara (1902–3), Ashur (1903–14) and Uruk (1928–39).
Jena, Friedrich-Schiller-Universität, Hilprecht Sammlung – tablets from the University of Philadelphia's excavations at Nippur.

Iraq
Baghdad, The Iraq Museum – tablets from all Iraqi excavations and many foreign excavations from 1920 onwards.

Italy
Aosta, Collegiata dei SS. Pietro e Orso.
Florence, Archaeological Museum.
Rome, Vatican Museum.

Netherlands
Leiden, University of Leiden, Böhl Collection.

Switzerland
Geneva, Musée d'Art et d'Histoire.

Syria
Aleppo National Museum – tablets from Ebla.
Damascus, The National Museum – tablets from Mari and Ugarit.

Turkey
Ankara, Museum of Anatolian Civilisations – Old Assyrian tablets from Kanesh and Hittite tablets from Hattuṣas.
Antakya, Hatay Museum – tablets from Alalah.
Istanbul, Archaeological Museums (Ancient Orient Museum) – tablets from various excavations in Mesopotamia conducted by foreign institutions during the time of the Ottoman Empire. Over 85,000 tablets in total.

UK
Birmingham, City Museums and Art Gallery.
Edinburgh, Royal Scottish Museum.
Liverpool, Merseyside County Museum.
London, British Museum – tablets from excavations at Kalhu (Nimrud) (1845–1963), Nineveh (1846–1932), Babylon and Sippar (1879–82), Tell ed-Der (1890–1), Ur (1922–34) and Alalah (1937–49), etc., and large collections acquired by purchase. Over 130,000 in total.
Manchester, The Manchester Museum.
Oxford, The Ashmolean Museum – tablets from excavations at Jemdet Nasr and Kish (1923–33).

USA
Ann Arbor, University of Michigan Museum.

Baltimore, The Walters Art Gallery.
Berkeley, University of California, Lowie Museum of Anthropology.
Cambridge, Harvard University, The Semitic Museum – tablets from Nuzi (1927–31).
Chicago, Oriental Institute Museum–tablets from Nippur (1948–), Eshnunna, (1930–37), etc. Over 20,000 tablets in total.
New Haven, Yale University – over 30,000 tablets.
New York, Columbia University Libraries.
New York, General Theological Seminary (E. A. Hoffman Collection).

New York, Metropolitan Museum of Art.
Philadelphia, Free Library.
Philadelphia, University Museum of the University of Pennsylvania – tablets from Nippur (1889–1900), Ur (1922–34), etc. Over 30,000 tablets in total.
Towson, Md., Goucher College.
Urbana, University of Illinois, World Heritage Museum.

USSR
Leningrad, State Hermitage Museum.
Moscow, State Pushkin Museum of Fine Arts.

39 A pre-Sargonic tablet from Girsu; a census of sheep from the time of king Uruinimgina (2351–2342 BC). BM 96591.

Further Reading

B. André-Leicknam and C. Ziegler, *Naissance de l'écriture*. Paris, 1982 (catalogue of an exhibition, containing a wealth of illustrations)

C. Bermant and M. Weitzman, *Ebla: an archaeological enigma*. London, 1979 (contains an excellent chapter on the decipherment of cuneiform)

E. Chiera, *They wrote on clay*. Chicago, 1938; reprinted 1975

A. Curtis, *Ugarit (Ras Shamra)*. Cambridge, 1985

G. R. Driver, *Semitic writing from pictograph to alphabet* (The Schweich Lectures of the British Academy 1944). Third revised edition, London, 1976

R. G. Kent, *Old Persian: Grammar, Texts, Lexicon*. New Haven, 1950

O. R. Gurney, *The Hittites*. Penguin Books, Harmondsworth, UK, 1981

W. Hinz, *The Lost World of Elam*. London, 1972

S. N. Kramer, *The Sumerians*. Chicago, 1963

A. L. Oppenheim, *Ancient Mesopotamia*. Revised edition, Chicago, 1977

G. Pettinato, *The Archives of Ebla: An Empire Inscribed in Clay*. Garden City, New York, 1981

É Puech, 'Origine de l'alphabet', *Revue Biblique* 93/2, 161–213 (Paris, April 1986)

World Archaeology 17/3: Early writing systems (Henley-on-Thames, February 1986) [a summary of recent research into the origins of writing]

Index

Figure numbers are in italic type.